From Smock To Cassock

With best wishes
to Robert and Stef.
From Cherry Tree Cottage
your Former home!

Michael G. Bishop

From Smock To Cassock

✦

My Personal Journey

Michael G. Bishop

iUniverse, Inc.
New York Lincoln Shanghai

From Smock To Cassock
My Personal Journey

iUniverse books may be ordered through booksellers or by contacting:

iUniverse
2021 Pine Lake Road, Suite 100
Lincoln, NE 68512
www.iuniverse.com
1-800-Authors (1-800-288-4677)

ISBN-13: 978-0-595-43224-0 (pbk)
ISBN-13: 978-0-595-87565-8 (ebk)
ISBN-10: 0-595-43224-7 (pbk)
ISBN-10: 0-595-87565-3 (ebk)

Printed in the United States of America

To Emma Joan Bishop, my granddaughter.

Contents

Introduction

I was born on June 9, 1927 only nine years after the signing of the Armistice which had ended the First World War, and twelve years before the awesome morning on September 3, 1939 when I would hear the sad and weary voice of Prime Minister Neville Chamberlain announce that Great Britain was at war with Hitler's Germany.

My father, Edward Roy Lennox Bishop, was the youngest son of Colonel Edward Barry Bishop and Louise Lamb. Colonel Bishop and his father both served in the Indian Army, and my grandfather was Colonel of the famous Gurkha regiment.

Roy, as he was known, had served his country as an officer in the Regular Army during the First World War. Destined to follow in the steps of his father and serve in India he transferred into the Kings Own Scottish Borderers with whom he saw action in the trenches in Belgium and France. He was seriously wounded, and posted as being 'missing believed killed while in action' in France. His story, as my mother told me many years later, was that he had been bayoneted in hand-to-hand fighting in the 'No Man's Land' (the area between the trenches) and left for dead. British troops had recovered the lost ground during a counter attack and he had been able to raise his arm and attract their attention to his plight. He returned to England only to find himself in action again during the I.R.A. troubles in Southern Ireland during the 1920's.

Later, as the British Armed Forces were disbanded, he, like so many other Officers and men who had survived the horrors and dangers of the Great War, and in which millions of young men on both sides of the melee had died in action, tramped the streets of London looking for a civilian job and career.

Roy's mother, my Granny Bishop, was a member of the Lamb family who once lived in Lamb House in Rye in East Sussex. My mother married him when he was a young lieutenant. She encouraged and supported him as eventually he began to build a new future as a journalist. Beginning as a reporter with the Western Morning News in Bristol, his new profession led them out to Malaya where he became Assistant Editor of the Malay Straits Times, based in Kuala Lumpur.

My mother, Dorothy Tytler, came from a Scottish family closely related to the Fraser Clan. She had spent much of her life as a young woman in India where her father, my grandfather Tytler, had served in the British Indian Army. His father, William 'Delhi-force' Tytler is said to have been born in a wagon during the historic siege of Delhi!

The impending birth of my brother Edward had eventually brought Roy and Dorothy home to England. With nowhere to set up home, a friend, Michael Holyrod, an Oxford Don who had inherited his family home, had kindly invited my parents to make this house their home. Known as Sturdie House, the home was situated in the fashionable area known as St. George's Hill, Oatlands Park, Weybridge, in Surrey. Sturdie House could be theirs at least until the safe arrival of their first child. My brother Edward was born three years my senior on May 5th 1924.

My earliest memory is from our time at Sturdie House. I recall lying in my pram parked beneath a towering cedar tree, gazing up at the gathering storm clouds. As the first raindrops came, they summoned up my ever faithful and watchful nanny. The canvas cover and hood of my pram was pulled into place. Then, as if in a hurried race, I was wheeled into the security of the kitchen. I was safely home.

The household staff could create that awareness of love which was, and still is to me, the most precious element in life. I felt secure in the company of the kitchen people. Perhaps they suppressed their unkind words and quarrels when young Michael was about, but in doing so they created a safe haven for me.

Cook and the housemaids referred to themselves as 'the servants'. The relationship between them and my parents was one of great respect. The class distinction between them was an accepted fact. This is the way that it was in England in those days. Little did I realise that I was experiencing the close of an era. The days of 'Master' Michael sharing the kitchen with the cook and maid servants, and in the care of his nanny, would soon be gone for ever.

Nanny Tangley, who had charge of both Edward and I, was the centre of our lives. The nursery in Sturdie House was my ultimate place of sanctuary. Although I adored my mother, my love for Nanny was unique. Nanny possessed a special purity. She brought fun, peace, and order into my early life.

Although I had been wonderfully loved by my mother, who in her later years became known to Edward and me as 'Moo', it was Nanny Tangley who was at the centre of my life during my early childhood.

I experienced a kind of bereavement for the first time when Nanny left us. She went away to marry her Salvation Army husband. I spent a last weekend with her and her husband at their home in Hearne Bay. Dressed now as a member of the Salvation Army, she looked very sweet and smart in her uniform and bonnet.

I last saw her marching with the band and praising Jesus. The experience excited me and made a lasting impression. They say that Christian faith takes root from the seeds of faith that are sown in a person's heart and mind. It happens secretly and the sowing goes unobserved until at the right time and place the seed germinates and begins to grow.

It seems that a mustard seed of faith was sown in the heart of the young Michael as he listened to the band and heard the word of God proclaimed by God's warriors, the Salvation Army.

Unaware of the seed's presence, and having to go out and earn my living at the tender age of fifteen, I donned a milking smock in a cow barn in East Sussex on March 2, 1942. I was to exchange it for a cassock on the day of my ordination as a Deacon in the Church of England in the great Cathedral at Gloucester on Trinity Sunday in 1965. This is the story of that pilgrimage.

Unhappy School Days

John Alexander, Junior Master and Music Teacher at Langley Place Preparatory School in Sussex, was at the point of exasperation. This stupid boy, known as 'Bishop Two', was obviously gifted, but he seemed to be completely unable to grasp the elementary skill of reading music. The edge of the ruler crashed on my slender knuckles, my hands became numb, the notes on the piano became even more cacophonic and, as always, the tears began to flow.

My inability to learn to read music, or even simple English, coupled with my insistence that I could only write using my left hand evoked a strange mixture of love and cruelty. How could it be that this boy could play all the popular tunes of the day on the piano by ear, and even do quite interesting improvisations, and yet be incapable of playing from the music? On one occasion unobserved by me, Mr. Alexander had stood in the doorway of the music room listening to me playing a popular tune of that period and singing the lyric, "Little old lady passing by, catching everyone's eye, she's a pretty picture in her lavender and lace." He had stormed angrily into the room and slammed down the lid of the piano. I had no time in which to rescue my fingers. I can only suppose that his well intentioned determination to make me use my gift of music erupted into this violent behaviour. I spent much of my time during the day, and in my bed in the dormitory, in tears. On one occasion, when I had burst into tears during a rehearsal for a school concert, the whole school, singing gleefully under the direction of Mr. Alexander, serenaded me with the words "poor little water butt". The tune was taken from Gilbert and Sullivan's opera Mikado and the song 'Dear Little Buttercup'!

My happiest moments were spent in the school chapel where Old Ted, the headmaster's brother, did his best to introduce us to God. Dressed in the Church of England's traditional cassock, surplice, scarf and an Oxford Master of Arts academic hood, he preached Sunday by Sunday throughout the school term. I can't remember anything that he said, but I recall him with affection. He was a kindly man and could make us listen and laugh. I have little doubt that he, like Nanny Tangley, was a sower of seeds of a spiritual nature. I loved the ancient hymns, and the Anglican chants for the psalms, and longed to be invited to join the choir. But I could not read either the words or the music and so the invitation never came. If God was working his purpose out, as one of my favourite hymns declared, I was to have little part to play in his plan. He appeared not to notice or respond to the tears of a small boy.

My brother Edward, a senior, who inhabited the school's heavens, embodied by being a member of the top form and even receiving invitations to partake of cream buns at the home of Old Ted from time to time! He was a great help to me despite, I'm sure, experiencing embarrassment concerning my backwardness. He persevered in teaching me the basic skills needed to survive my early days at school. He was very impatient with me. He wondered how his brother had evaded the notice of the whole family and come to boarding school without having learnt the elementary skills of caring for his personal appearance. His fingers are always inky, his hair never tidy, he was constantly reduced to tears, and worst of all he was frequently reported to have wet his bed. Despite all this, he stood by me when I needed help, and in times of despair.

My one success was to take place on the cricket field. I loved the sound of bat on ball and sight of the greenery of the cricket ground set in the Sussex countryside. The purchase of my first cricket bat and a pair of white flannel trousers were major events for me. The smell of linseed oil still evokes the pleasure and excitement of smoothing the oil onto the surface of the wooden bat, which was made from willow. I was proud to take the field wearing long trousers for the first time. The transition from short trousers to long was a major step up the ladder of the school hierarchy!

I looked forward to the school holidays when I would go home to 'High Chimneys'. Although the family had the usual ups and downs, and I certainly contributed to them by throwing fits of bad temper and tantrums, these were happy days at our much loved home in Sussex. High Chimneys in Whatlington, near Battle, had been a farm house. My parents had rented it from the local Vicar's wife, who was also a farmer. She owned Ringlets Farm nearby where she bred goats, Angora rabbits, and Jersey cows. The meadows, which surrounded High Chimneys and the way of life on the farm, fascinated me. I loved to watch the cows as they grazed on the rich Sussex pastures. With full stomachs, they would collapse onto the ground in an ungainly way and, with a contented sigh, regurgitate their feed of grass and chew the cud displaying humorous expressions of bovine contentment. Regularly each day the herd would make their way to the farm yard and into the cowsheds for milking. I enjoyed following them and watching them being milked.

My initiation into the farming business came with the gift of twelve Hoed Island Red hens. I then bought a wooden hen house which was specially designed so that the production of eggs from each hen could be recorded. The hen would enter a nest when moved to produce her daily egg. A trap door would ensure that she could only be released when her egg was collected. I named each of my hens. A favourite of mine was Clara Cluck. I would record Clara and her fellow hens' production of eggs in a note book. I was enchanted by the busy-ness of the 'girls', their joy at the moment of egg production and their eventual release into the wired run in which they resided. Their eggs were to become part of my contribution to the war. I would sell the eggs to neighbours. They earned me my first small farming income being worth just a few pence each. It was a fortune to me, but this effort foreshadowed my future career.

The large lawn at High Chimneys was equipped with practice nets for cricket. As we practiced batting and bowling on those lovely summer holidays we were aware of Pop's concern over the rapidly deteriorating situation between Britain and Germany. Pops, having served in the army during the First World War (1914-1918) as a regular officer in the Kings Own Scottish Borderers, was anxious. As the situation worsened, he began to fear that he might once again be called to take up arms and serve in the army. Meanwhile he enjoyed playing cricket with us. Edward developed considerable skill as a fast bowler, and who else could he practice on but me! I therefore gained experience as a batsman. As a bowler I was less fortunate. For some reason I was quite unable to learn how to bowl over arm, although being left handed I had a talent for causing the ball to spin ferociously. Bowling under arm, as one learns to do in the early days of playing cricket, I became expert at puzzling and entrapping the batsmen.

There was a moment of great fulfilment when, back at school, my bowling was called upon by Dubbo, the affectionate nickname for Mr. Roberts, Headmaster of Langley Place School. Edward was the captain of a school team which had been named 'The Episcopalians'. He had been amassing a huge score, and I was fielding as a very junior member of the opposing team that day. After my brother had hit yet another 'four' off the ineffective bowling of the school's second best bowler (Edward was the best) there was a shout from Mr. Roberts who was watching the game from the pavilion. "Put on little Bishop." This was the equivalent of a divine command. The captain of my team threw me the ball. "You have a go." He said petulantly. There were derisive giggles from all the players, and onlookers. My brother glared at me from his exalted position at the further end of the pitch. I ran in, and delivered a perfect length off break. To my own astonishment, and the mirth of the headmaster and staff in the pavilion I heard the wonderful sound of the ball hitting the stumps. I observed the bails fly up into the air. I had bowled him out. The school's score book read 'Bishop One, bowled Bishop Two'. Edward made his furious way back into the pavilion. That was one of only a very few moments of triumph as a school boy.

Having accomplished the task of teaching me such elementary skills as to how to tie my school tie correctly, Edward abandoned me to make my own way through my school days. I slowly adjusted to life in a boarding school and he moved on to his Public School at Clifton College.

The school swimming pool was the scene for my second moment of fame. Swimming lessons were compulsory. Wearing a harness which was attached to a rope held by the retired Sergeant Major who supervised physical training, boxing, and swimming the younger boys would be half drowned as they floundered desperately to keep afloat. One day, quite soon after I had passed the test which allowed swimming without the aid (or hindrance) of the harness I was first in the pool when the head master's Pekingese dog, aided by a well concealed kick from one of the seniors, fell into the pool. The poor little dog was yapping and snarling in panic. Despite its efforts to evade me, I managed to grab it under its furry little tummy and deliver its wet and wriggling body onto dry land at the side of the pool. I was cheered by the astonished onlookers.

Later I was thanked by a grateful Head and rewarded with lemonade and a cream bun in his study. The only other time that I had been in this awesome room was when I was expecting to be caned. The use of corporal punishment was a normal procedure in schools, and few pupils escaped without at least one beating during their time at school.

As the dark clouds of impeding war gathered we were unaware that our lives would soon be subjected to real and traumatic change. These days of peace would all too soon be over.

The changes came upon us very rapidly. Edward had to leave Clifton College, and my days at Langley Place were ended too as the outbreak of war and the mobilization of Britain's armed forces reclaimed Lieutenant Roy Bishop. Army pay could not maintain two boys at private schools.

I can discern that despite my unhappiness at Langley Place, my experiences there created a foundation of self-dependence which would be of immense value to me in the years ahead. Above all I learned how to survive in adversity and how to work hard. The education that I received at Langley Place was destined to be the only academic schooling of any significance that I would get. Despite learning self-dependence, I was endowed with a deep sense of insecurity, and had difficulty in overcoming intense shyness and self-consciousness.

A Literary Career Cut Short

The coming of war was a far greater tragedy for my father. In the years prior to the Second World War, Roy and Dorothy enjoyed a busy social life. Bridge parties and the Tennis Club filled their days. During these years he strove to build up his life as a journalist and author. In time he expanded his interests into the fields of publicity and arranging art exhibitions. One of his principal art exploits had been the mounting of an art gallery on board the transatlantic liner RMS Berengaria for Lord Joseph Duveen, and holding the exhibition aboard the liner whilst anchored in New York harbour.

My father's one published book, 'Paintings of the Royal Collection', was causing great interest when the outbreak of the Second World War occurred. But unfortunately the war was to destroy this evolving and distinguished career. He would accept the call to serve his country cheerfully and bravely, knowing full well that his career as an author and journalist had only recently begun to bear fruit after long years of patient work and research.

'Paintings of the Royal Collection' was the prize jewel in the crown of his pre-war achievements. The book was published by George G. Harrap and Co. Ltd in the year 1937. Within its pages was contained the first information ever made public concerning the rich collection of paintings which adorn the Royal Palaces. Pops had experienced great difficulty in obtaining permission to visit the Royal Family's private apartments in the palaces. Permission had been granted by King Edward VIII. The King's abdication on December 11, 1936 made it necessary for the whole process of obtaining permission to be undertaken for a second time. King George VI graciously endorsed his brother's decision and so the project was put back on track. The survey of His Majesty's pictures at Windsor Castle, Buckingham Palace, Hampton Court, Holyrood House and Balmoral stands as a fit memorial to its author. The book's dedication reads: *To his Majesty the King, who has given his Gracious permission for this book to be written and for paintings of the Royal Collection to be reproduced and who granted exceptional facilities for the author to visit and work in the Royal Palaces, the author asks respectfully to be permitted to express his profound feelings of loyalty and gratitude.*

The book caused tremendous interest and spurred invitations for a series of lecture tours accumulated from across the nation. Most excitingly of all, Her Majesty Queen Mary, the Queen Mother, requested that he would present his lecture to her. It was to be held at Londonderry House in London. This invitation was very quickly accepted. We were invited to attend as a family and informed that we should be prepared to be presented to her Majesty.

The great day arrived. We made camp, appropriately at the Rembrandt Hotel in Knightsbridge. Moo later claimed that the Lounge was turned into a slum by the Bishop family! As we waited for a taxi to take us to Londonderry House it was noticed that I needed smartening up. I was examined, and double checked, for the least vestige of hen manure, and (as still happens to this day) my hair defied all attempts to be made tidy. We all had to be very quiet so that Pops could be kept calm. Soon we were on our way to Londonderry House.

As we took our seats, I could see no sight of the Queen. We were kept standing for a long time before we were told that we could take our seats. The Queen had arrived and the lecture was about to begin. I was very proud to see my father as he stepped forward to introduce his lantern slides which were the first pictures of the Royal Collection ever to be produced in colour. As the lecture progressed it was clear that it was being well received, there was polite laughter at times, and Pop's excellent speaking voice held the attention of his Royal audience. Quite suddenly it was all over. We were ordered to remain in our seats. Queen Mary had requested that we should all go forward to be presented to her.

A broadly smiling and relaxed looking Pops appeared in the centre aisle, and beckoned to us. After a walk down a long corridor we were given our instructions. We were not on any account to speak first but we should be ready to answer Her Majesty's questions. When it was time to leave we should take three steps backward before turning around and walking out of the room. "How shall we know when we have to go?" I asked.

Her Majesty's Lady in Waiting gave me a knowing look. "Oh, you'll know. The Queen makes it quite plain when she wants her visitors to leave."

Her Majesty looked very beautiful. She was quite tall and I can still remember being held in awe by the bright glistening of her jewels. Questions were addressed to the whole family. At the question 'Where did we live?' the family seemed to be leaving the giving of the answer to me. Being the youngest, I had been unable to get a word in. On hearing that we lived in East Sussex she exclaimed, "That's one of my favourite places!" She then asked me, "Do you know Bodiam Castle?"

Feeling at ease with my new friend, I replied "We love to go to Bodiam."

The Queen looked delighted and said, "When I come to Sussex again, I'll call for you and we will go to Bodiam Castle for a picnic." Then after a short time of further conversation the time for dismissal came. Queen Mary made it abundantly clear by her demeanour that it was time for us to leave. Pops, Moo and Edward took three steps backwards before turning to make their way out of the Queen's presence. For me it was to be a moment of catastrophe. Having backed away for two steps I lost my balance and fell over. Regaining my feet, I raced back down the corridor as fast as I could run. The picnic at Bodiam was never to be.

The situation in Europe continued deteriorating on a daily basis. During these last few months before the war a letter was also received from Herr Von Ribbentrop who was in charge of Foreign Affairs in the government of Adolph Hitler. Hitler himself had requested that the lecture be given before him; such was his interest in these British treasures! The Foreign Office told Pops that he must on no account go to Berlin to present the lecture to Adolph Hitler.

He also received an invitation to tour the United States of America. A lecture tour of the States, with his lantern slides, was cancelled only a few weeks prior to the outbreak of war. What was likely a prelude to rising fortune for the family, soon collapsed.

Since Pops had seen active service during World War One, I thought one war must be enough for any man. However, my dad was to experience active service for a second time!

A few months before the declaration of war in 1939, Roy, now forty-three years old, was recalled into the Army since he was still eligible for military service. It was only twenty-one years after the ending of the Great War of 1914-1918. Adorned once more in his uniform as a Lieutenant in the Kings Own Scottish Borderers he described himself as the fattest Lieutenant in the British Army. Back in uniform, he soon resumed his training and military duties.

I was only 12 years old when we were all together in High Chimneys on September 3, 1939 and heard Prime Minister Neville Chamberlain tell the Nation that we were now at war with Germany.

My father's departure across the English Channel to France only a few months before the dispatch of the full British Expeditionary Force is engraved in my memory. We were driven in our old Morris Oxford family car to a position high up on the white cliffs of Dover. From there we watched his troopship sail away. We stayed for as long as we could follow the ship's progress as she covered the short voyage between England and France.

Daffodils and Bombs

Pops served as an officer in the British Intelligence. He found that the rigours of the very severe winter in that first year of war proved to be too harsh for him. The story is far from clear but it seems that he, together with some younger officers and men, had been keeping watch on a farm house which was located across the French border in Belgium. Belgium was still a neutral country at this time. Some German agents were thought to be hiding out there. Lying in the deep snows and frozen by the bitter winds of that first winter, which became known as 'the phoney war', he had realised that he could no longer move his legs. The lower half of his body was paralyzed. His companions dragged him a considerable distance to the safety of their French hideout. Eventually he found his way into the care of the doctors. Soon thereafter he was transported back to England and cared for at Park Prewett Hospital, near Basingstoke in Hampshire.

Moo, who had been unaware of this dramatic turn in his life, had in time been called to visit him. I find it hard to imagine the anguish they went through together as he struggled to overcome his problems and regain his health. He had, she told me, to learn how to walk all over again.

In time psychiatric help and physiotherapy had brought a wonderful measure of healing. Throughout all these troubles he had never lost his immense sense of humour. He once described how he had delighted in outwitting the 'trick cyclists' as he called his doctors. He claimed that he had at one point convinced them that he thought he was an elephant! His ability to tell highly imaginative stories very convincingly never deserted him. Tragically he was never to be really well again.

The change in our family's fortunes had by now released me from the awesome and unhappy life that I had suffered at Preparatory School. With the future so uncertain, many of the other pupils at Langley Place School had been moved to the safety of a location in Canada. I stayed in Battle, Sussex. A town so named because it was the site of the Battle of Hastings in 1066. My education continued there, temporarily under the direction of the Reverend John Catterick, Assistant Curate to the Dean of Battle, the Very Reverend W. W. Youard.

My companions at this makeshift school were the sons of Malcolm and Kitty Muggeridge. The Muggeridge family was in a similar predicament to ours. Malcolm had also been called up for active duty. The two neighbours, who had both been following a literary career, became close friends. Malcolm was later to become world famous as an author, journalist and television celebrity. The Muggeridge boys and I made an irreligious, but happy group of scholars. Neither of our families was closely attached to the Church, and I have often wondered how this little school came into being. The interval of happy and fulfilled days in the Curate's care was a time of happiness. My lack of self confidence receded and my sense of worth and achievement increased day after day. In addition to our time in class we were given various tasks. One such task was to raise money for Lord Beaverbrook's appeal to the nation to provide funds with which to build Spitfire fighter planes. We made our own small contribution to the eventual winning of the great air battle, known as the Battle of Britain, by picking all the daffodils we could find in the Church, Rectory and Curate's gardens, and selling them to all our friends and neighbours.

Moo's war effort had been gallant. Enrolled as a member of the Women's Voluntary Services (WVS) she drove an ambulance in Hastings. The town had become a front line of defence as it is situated only eighty miles from the coast of France. There were frequent attacks by marauding Luftwaffe planes that straggled the town with bombs and sometimes strafed the sea promenade with machine-gun bullets. On one occasion while she was on ambulance duty, I went with her to Hastings to enjoy a walk beside the sea. I experienced war first hand as I was forced to take cover as bullets hummed and ricocheted along the Promenade from Luftwaffe planes overhead.

At this time, my grandmother, Emma Louise Bishop, was in her eighties. She moved from the Channel Island of Jersey, which had been the home of my father's parents, to live in St. Leonard's in order to be near the family. On one occasion a machine gun bullet had become embedded in the wall behind her bed. She maintained afterwards that the plane had been flying so low that she had actually heard the German bomber pilot breathing!

During this intense time an incident took place which was to influence my choice of job when that time came for me to go out into the world and earn my own living. I always enjoyed and found interest in attending the busy cattle market in Battle. This was the weekly meeting of the local farming community. The Market was a noisy, dirty, and busy place. The farmers would arrive with their cattle, and other livestock which were to be sold by auction. The action and the language were rough and tough, and totally different from anything I had come across in my life so far. I was fascinated by this other world from which I had been sheltered until now.

One day, as I lent over a wooden rail watching the calves, and listened to their pathetic lowing as they were herded into pens to await their future on the airy and beef farms of England, a man shouted at me. He was wearing a filthy khaki coat, the coat being held around his ample waist by a scruffy piece of string. "Here boy. D'ye want to earn a few bob?" Before I had decided to answer yes or no he shoved a bucket filled with strong smelling glue into my hand. He passed an old paint brush and a packet of numbered labels into my free hand. "Stick them labels on them calves," he commanded.

There was nothing else to do but comply. I jumped over the rail into the midst of the calves. My feet were stamped on and I nearly slipped beneath the seething mass of terrified animals that were moving around trying to make space for themselves in the overcrowded enclosure. I struggled on until each calf displayed a number on its back.

My employer was delighted. "Well done m'boy," he said. A shining half-crown was pressed into the palm of my hand. Polluted by the stinking manure which had been swarmed onto my person and my clothing by the unfortunate calves, I made my way home to High Chimneys.

On arrival Moo looked horrified when I appeared before her. "What on earth have you been doing?" she exclaimed.

"I've been at work," I replied as I flourished my hard earned coin before her. She declined to make any further comment, but suggested that I take off my clothes there and then and go and have a hot bath.

This short period of freedom, such as I had not experienced before, was to end with the return of Pops from hospital. We needed to move to London to be near the work to which he had been appointed after a long and anxious time of job hunting. The fact that he had been discharged from the army as being 'unfit for further military service' had not been helpful. Happily, he had now secured an interesting position as a Press Liaison Officer, working for the Ministry of Information, based in the building which now houses the University of London. This was where the world Press Corps assembled in order to hear the official news of the progress of the war. The Press Liaison Officer's job was to make the announcements which they had previously approved after having subjected them to a careful examination and censorship. He was at last happy in his work.

More trouble lay ahead though as the bombing of London was about to begin. Our family was moving into town just as all those who could do so were evacuating and going to live in safer places in the surrounding countryside! As predicted, it wasn't long before Hitler's massive bombing attacks on our British capital began.

The Blitzkrieg

My Godfather, Michael Holroyd, had provided a roof over our heads by lending us Sturdie House in the early 1930's. Now a friend of Pops offered his London home to us. Number 8, Campden Hill Square, the property of a Mr. Graham Rawson, was offered to us. Campden Hill Square is a prestigious neighbourhood situated off Holland Park Avenue in West London. Arriving from the beauty of our home in Sussex, the sight of the trees, shrubs and grass in the typical London square in front of our new home was reassuring. The house, three stories high, looked elegant although the outside decoration was showing signs of neglect. Inside, the rooms on the ground floor were shrouded in dust sheets. Climbing the stairs we were met with the same rather desolate scene. Peeping beneath the covers we discovered antique furniture, a harpsichord and valuable pictures. A further narrow flight of stairs led upwards to the top floor. This is where the servants would have had their quarters. It was clean and comfortable and merely needed dusting in order to become habitable. We set to work to set up our new home.

The home's owner, Graham Rawson, was a friend of my parents. He had agreed that we could use the house in exchange for a peppercorn (nominal) rent. Our commitment was that we should do our best to save the house from being burned down. London was to come under attack from Adolph Hitler's Luftwaffe, the German Air Force. Fire and high explosive bombs would likely be showered on London.

When the 'blitzkrieg' came in late 1940, I was thirteen years old. The spirit of the English people was incredibly strong despite the fear the blitz caused. Londoners from every walk of life and social background were joined together as one united family of citizens. There was nothing that could be done if a high explosive bomb should make a hit on or nearby our home, but it might be possible to tackle an incendiary bomb if it fell onto our roof.

We kept our contract on a memorable night which, as it happened, was also one of the last occasions when our family was to be together. The night was dark and clear. The warning sirens had wailed soon after dark and the hum-hum of bombers could be clearly discerned. Next the anti-aircraft guns opened up. The noise was frightening. An explosion and the severe shaking of the house persuaded Pops that it was time to inspect the roof top. An incendiary bomb had fallen onto our roof. The scenes around us were devastating. Smoke and fire could be seen in every direction. We shovelled sand onto the bomb and soaked it with water, as we had been trained to do by the Civil Defence Corps. Then Pops courageously approached it armed with a long handled shovel and launched it off the roof into the back garden. Our rent had been paid, and Number Eight is still there to this day!

The awesome sight from the roof showed us that the Kensington area of London was on fire. Smoke and flames engulfed Church Street, Kensington, and much of the surrounding district. London's fire fighters, professional and amateur, along with every able bodied citizen who could help, were doing their best to tackle the flames which seemed to encompass the capital. But it was obvious that the situation was out of control. A hasty family conference having been held, Moo reluctantly agreed that Pops, and her two sons should venture out into the streets to see if we could help too.

In Church Street, where the fire which was rapidly spreading from house to house, we noticed flames beginning to take hold on a roof that had so far escaped the inferno. Ordering us to stay near him Pops rang the door bell. After a short interval an elderly man, who looked as if he might have been a butler opened the door.

"I'm afraid your roof is on fire! My we come in and try to deal with it?" Pops seemed very calm and the polite way in which he asked the question seemed to me to be quite humorous.

The good manners of old England were not to be omitted despite the dangerous situation. Having filled our buckets with water and sand which were always nearby for use in case of emergency, we hastened up the well carpeted staircase. I tripped and the bucket of water cascaded down the stairs. Having raced back to the kitchen to refill my bucket I made my way to the roof, where the fire was already extinguished. Pops and Edward bravely repeated our roof top rescue of Number Eight by scooping the flaming bomb over the edge of the parapet. I could see it burning away ineffectively in the yard below.

Further down the street another house was well ablaze. We were obviously too late to be of any use. Looking through a window we could see that an elderly man was desperately attempting to rescue a large painting. The front door was open. Impulsively I rushed inside.

Pops was yelled desperately, "Come back Michael. Come back there's nothing we can do."

But I was already committed. As I entered the room I saw to my horror that the ceiling was collapsing. It came down with a great thump, and the heat and smoke and red hot cinders became unbearable. I saw the poor man, whoever he was, clutching his painting. He was engulfed by the flames and crashing timbers as the house fell in on him. Only just in time, I made my retreat to the cooler but smoke ridden air of the street. I had failed to save his life. Who was he and what was the painting? We wondered, and sadly made our way home.

An angry but proud father and brother made their feelings very clear to me. I had been reckless in entering the inferno and was lucky to have escaped injury, or death, but they phrased it in rather more colourful language than that! They were right. If I had been a few yards further into the room it would have been the end of my story.

In the following days, the thoughts of my parents turned to the need to get me back to school. Pitman's Commercial College, in Southampton Row, Holborn offered various courses for enrolment. Although I was young compared with most of the other students, I was accepted. The plan was that I should be prepared and qualified to take a job as soon as was practicable.

My father had contacts in Fleet Street, and hoped that I would be interested in following him and my brother Edward into journalism. The subjects selected for me were English, Double Entry Book Keeping, Pitman's Shorthand and Typewriting. Armed with the confidence engendered by Mr. Catteries's make-shift school in Battle, I entered into my new schooling with enthusiasm. The daily journey from Holland Park Tube Station to Holborn had the effect of making me feel very grown up. I was very proud to be able to flourish my season ticket each time I entered the station.

By night these same tube stations often became the refuge of many Londoners. Bunk beds were fixed in tiers along the platforms for those who had been bombed out of home, together with anxious young families whose children had remained in London. By morning they would be making their way up into the open air after their night in the deep shelter. Many would sadly find that their homes were no longer in existence when they returned to their bomb ravaged streets.

Social life was limited to our regular visits to the local pub, just across the street in Holland Park Avenue. Granny Bishop who had followed the family to London was now settled into a Residential Home. Her bedroom window overlooked the pub. Being a devout member of the Scottish Presbyterian Church she disapproved of our regular visits there. We would have to slip in through the door when we could see that she was not watching. Pops and Moo were regularly to be found in the bar. Edward and I had been introduced to beer drinking at an early age. The pub became the place to meet and talk things over.

There were concrete shelters, which could be used for day time emergencies on many of London's streets. These too were crammed with families each night. An Air Raid Warden would be on duty at each shelter, and he was sometimes assisted by a member of the Cadet Forces. One evening as I made my way home from Pitman's College I noticed a very smart young man of my own age wearing the uniform of a Seaman in the Royal Navy standing at the entrance to a shelter. His hat band bore the words 'Sea Cadet Corps'. I stopped to talk to him to enquire how one could join the Sea Cadets. He invited me round to their North Kensington headquarters.

Later that evening I attended their parade night and saw how they were being trained to take their places in the Royal Navy when they were old enough. Every British boy had to register his name for entry into the armed forces on his eighteenth birthday. If I joined the cadet force, I reasoned, it would prepare me for that day, and I would avoid basic training on entry. I watched the boys muster and the hoisting of the Royal Navy's flag, the White Ensign, as they began their evening's training. They were learning how to tie knots and coil ropes, how to march and salute, and also the elementary rules of navigation and astronomy. There was tuition and help in improving their maths too.

I enlisted and was assigned to a class led by Lieutenant Hay. Little did I know that my officer was in fact a famous actor. Will Hay was a very famous comedian, and starred in a number of humorous movies made by the Ealing Film Studios. You can still see them sometimes today when they show some of the old black and white movies of the 1940's. One of Will Hay's star roles was as a school teacher. He was in real life an excellent teacher and I enjoyed his classes. I was very proud to qualify and wear my sailor cadet's uniform. I had never mixed with boys from a working class background before. I enjoyed their wit and sense of humour. My accent, which they called 'posh', caused them to make fun of me. But they soon accepted me as one of the squad.

Unfortunately my time in the Sea Cadet Corps was to be short. Surgery became necessary for me to correct a physical fault which had been a problem to me throughout my childhood. This was a difficult subject for a shy person to talk about. The testicle on my right side had failed to descend into the scrotum when I was a child and now that I was reaching out towards maturity it had to be dealt with.

"Believe me," said the surgeon, "you'll be grateful to me and your parents in later life".

I was to be 'dealt with' in The Royal Northern Hospital, in Holloway Road. The Royal Northern looked desolate. Windows were either boarded up, or were crisscrossed with tape which was designed to prevent them from shattering and causing greater injury if a bomb should fall nearby. It was a foreboding place and the men's ward was packed with the victims of the bombing in addition to those who were in to have the more ordinary treatments and operations. The nurses were young, but were supervised by a very strict Ward Sister. The caring was excellent. As I was prepared for the operation, I was informed that when I awoke after the surgery I would find that I was tied to a splint. It was vitally important that I didn't move.

The night following the operation there was a big air raid. The other patients in the ward were evacuated to an underground shelter, but I was unable to go. A nurse was assigned to stay and take care of me. The noise was fearsome and the crunch of heavy explosives awesome. My nurse, whose name I never knew, but who I often wished I could meet again, held my hand and took care of me until the 'all clear' siren sounded at about 4 a.m. Shortly afterwards the ward began to re-assemble as the patients returned to their beds in the early morning light. A new nursing team took over and I was never to see my night nurse again. I believe that I had met an angel that night. Later in life I came across William Blake's poem which describes my experience that night so long ago. *'Love seeketh not itself to please nor for itself hath any care, but for another gives it's ease and builds a heaven in hell's despair.'* My nurse's example of unselfish love had been a thought provoking episode in my young life.

While I had difficulty in overcoming the embarrassment I felt concerning the operation, the surgery was successful; however, I have always experienced weakness on the right side of my body ever since. After a period of convalescence and a further period at Pitman's College, the time had come for me to do my part to ease the financial problems being experienced by the family and go to work to earn my own living.

Pops considered that my shorthand and typing were adequate, indeed, "quite good", and made an appointment for me to see the sub-editor of the London Evening Standard newspaper. There was an opening for a Cub Reporter. I would have to take a proficiency test in the newsroom to see if I would qualify. Very nervous, and tremendously excited, I made my way to the newspaper's office in Fleet Street. This part of London was a busy scene as the city's working life continued despite the ordeal being experienced through the days and nights of Hitler's relentless attacks.

Mr. Suhr, the Sub-Editor was a big and kind looking man. He invited me into his office and described the job that was awaiting me if I could pass the test. I would become a telephone reporter. I would have to use my shorthand to take messages and news stories down when they were called in. Then I would have to type up the information accurately and pass it on for his editorial team to see for possible inclusion in the evening newspaper.

Mr. Suhr began to dictate at what seemed to be a very fast pace. I wondered if I would ever be able to read back the wild strokes, dots and squiggles appearing on my notebook. I was in despair, when quite unexpectedly all my problems were resolved. As was becoming quite common during the day, the air raid sirens began to wail.

Mr. Suhr rose to his feet and raced across the office to a hat stand. He grabbed his tin helmet and gas mask, blew his whistle and turned hurriedly to me and bawled, "Take cover boy. Down to the shelters!"

The last that I saw of him was that of his burly figure shepherding his newsroom staff along the corridor. I could hear the 'akk akk' opening fire, and the familiar crunch of exploding bombs in the distance. I raced out into the street and down into the nearest tube train station to make my way home to Holland Park.

When Pops returned from his work that evening he was plainly excited to hear how I had got on. As he listened to my tale his face fell. "You mean to say," He said incredulously, "you just left the office and came home?" He was distressed and angry. No further effort was made to contact the London Evening News and I was not invited back to resume my interview. My career in journalism had already come to an end.

The Call of the Countryside

By early 1942, the smoke and dust of wartime London began to affect my health. As a young man of not quite fifteen years of age I must either be in school or start work.

"You must get this boy out into the country. He needs some good fresh air." The specialist in Harley Street was adamant. There was a very real fear that I might contract tuberculosis, the disease which was still dreaded in those days. The abortive adventure into Fleet Street and the world of journalism, along with my utter failure to comprehend book keeping raised questions about my employment opportunities. When coupled with the threat of tuberculosis my immediate future became a great concern to all of us. My parents could see no way out of the situation. I solved their problem myself in a most unexpected way.

I had seldom had deep or personal conversations with Pops. We seemed to be on different wavelengths much of the time except for the love and respect we shared between us. We had times of happiness, fun, and often shared the most atrocious jokes together. One Sunday morning he took me by surprise. "Mike" he began earnestly "You've got a few years before you, before they call you up for military service, and Mum and I don't think that you should stay in London. The doctor is very concerned about your cough and continuously bad chest. What would you like to do? Have you any ideas?"

I had been thinking things over for myself and had an answer ready. "I'd like to be a farmer," I said.

He stared at me in amazement. It was a family 'first'. His son, going in for farming! His reply, when it came, was typical and wonderful. "Then I'd better find out how we go about it," was all that he said.

I was not present when he broke the news to Moo. When she saw me later she had a mischievous smile on her face and said, "Pops is fixing up an interview with the Minister of Agriculture."

His maxim was 'always go straight to the top'. I had already abused his attempt to launch me into the world of newspapers. I wondered if I would let him down a second time in my choice of farming as a career.

Before long, Pops and I visited the Ministries building in Whitehall, London. There we met with the Right Honourable R.S. Hudson, Minister of Agriculture and Fisheries in Winston Churchill's wartime coalition government. Minister Hudson was responsible for getting Britain's farms mobilized to produce the vital and strategic quantity of food needed in time of war. When Pops finished explaining the circumstances to him, the man smiled benevolently and asked me why I wanted to be a farmer. I told him about my twelve hens and their egg production. Then I shared the story of my visit to the market in Battle.

"But have you ever worked on a farm?" He wondered.

"I've helped on Mrs. Browle's farm in Sussex in school holidays." I replied cheerfully.

"Sussex," he said with interest.

Making a note on his pad he told Pops "I think your best way forward will be to get a copy of the farming magazine, 'Farmer and Stockbreeder'. You'll see that some farmers are advertising vacancies for boys to work on their farms as pupils. Michael should test out his vocation by working on a farm for six months. If he still wants to go ahead, we will see if we can get him into the East Sussex School of Agriculture at Plumpton." Mr. Hudson continued making notes on his pad and continued, "I know the Principal, R.H.B. Jesse very well and I am sure that he will be able to give you further advice." He rose to his feet and shook hands with us both. We were then escorted to the door of his office.

My farming career had started at the top. We made our way home to Campden Hill Square, picking up a copy of 'Farmer and Stockbreeder' on the way. The farming magazine contained an advertisement which read, 'Gentleman Farmer requires pupil on small dairy farm in East Sussex'. There was a telephone number. Moo made the phone call and we were invited down for an interview at Broad Oak Farm, Chiddingly.

The train from Victoria Station, London had taken Moo and I to Lewes, the County town of East Sussex. From there we walked up a steep cobbled street to the High Street. There was a long queue for the Southdown bus that we needed to catch. When it arrived we were squashed in amongst all the country folk who had been doing their weekly shopping in the town.

As we asked the woman bus conductor for the tickets, a kind person nearby informed us, "You need to get off at the Bat and Ball. The farm lane's just where the bus stops."

The ride through the Sussex countryside made a pleasant change from the grime and dust of London in wartime. I enjoyed watching the Sussex farmers hard at work with their horses and farm implements. I soaked in the sight of the farm fields and the South Downs both looking as peaceful as ever. The fields were being ploughed and sown with wheat and barley. Other fields were scattered with the herds of cattle and flocks of sheep. The hedgerows that bordered the roads and separated the fields were just beginning to exhibit the first signs of spring time.

Before long the conductress shouted meaningfully, "Bat and Ball, next stop." We had arrived. There, just as had been described, was the farm lane. However, this particular lane was extremely muddy. We picked our way down it, initially seeing no sign of the farm house. To the right of our path lay a woodland pond and ahead the lane soon divided. One track led down towards a farm yard, but the left hand side, which became much less muddy, led to the door of a typical red brick Sussex farm house. I felt much more confident than I had for the interview at the London Evening News! This time I had Moo beside me, but even so my fears became acute as the front door opened. A buxom, middle aged woman, who turned out to be the farmer's wife, invited us in. First there was the customary cup of tea and then we were taken out to meet the farmer.

Mr. Fordham, who had described himself as a gentleman, was forking hay into some racks. The calves he was feeding looked rather friendlier than he did! "So, you're Michael. You've come highly recommended!" Did I detect a certain note of sarcasm in his voice, I wondered? Without wasting words he continued, "Can you start next week?"

Moo and I exchanged glances anxiously. "Yes Sir," I replied.

"But I'll have to get him some suitable clothes and boots," Moo said whilst looking down at my once shiny London shoes, and smart grey flannel trousers now badly stained with mud and cow dung.

"I'll see you on March 2nd then, about this time of day." Mr. Fordham had not mentioned anything about what the arrangements would be, about pay and time off. He paused for a few moments and then announced, "I'll give you five shillings a week pocket money, your keep, and one weekend off each month." Neither Pops, Moo nor I had received prior advice as to what the arrangement for payment should be. The offer sounded very little. But then, as I was described as a pupil, perhaps I would be like an apprentice learning his trade, so the deal was accepted and we made our way back to London.

I presented myself for work on March 2, 1942. I was fourteen years, and ten months old, and I felt very afraid, and desperately lonely.

A Boy in the Mud

When I arrived at the train station to depart for my work at Broad Oak Farm, I was carrying a dilapidated and bulging suitcase! The train was crowded with service men and women, many of whom were so exhausted that they slept lying full length along the train's corridors. Every seat was occupied, but the boy with the very large suitcase was tolerated with the kindness which was typical of the times. Great Britain was at war, and we were all in it together. The unpleasantness which was so evident in pre-war Britain had been replaced by a fellowship and camaraderie that introduced brightness into the stress and dreariness of life in a nation at war.

Upon arrival in Lewes, I struggled up the steep hill from the rail station to Lewes High Street. My suitcase felt heavier with every step. I joined the long queue for the Southdown bus. On arrival the bus was already almost full. Monday was Market Day in Lewes so the women's shopping bags and baskets were full. The small children were restless and fretful. The bus groaned its way heading for the bus stop near the farm known even today as 'The Bat and Ball'.

The farm lane was muddier than ever. This time it seemed more hazardous as I manhandled the suitcase which held my new farm clothes and Wellington boots. Mrs. Fordham greeted me at the front door, which I was to enter for the last time. She led me to the kitchen where a cup of hot, sweet tea was very welcome. The aroma of chicken roasting in the oven augured well for the future I thought. Checking the oven and seeing that I had finished my tea, Mrs. Fordham kindly invited me to follow her to my room.

"I'm afraid you won't be inside the house" she announced. "We run a guest house as well as the farm." We passed down a cold and damp corridor to the back door and out to a small yard littered with straggly pieces of straw and evidence that it was used regularly by the farm animals. I soon discovered I was about to become a fellow inhabitant with them!

Mrs. Fordham opened a door into a brick shed which she invited me to enter. This was to be my first independent home. There was a camp bed and a rough wooden box which had once transported oranges from South Africa. This crate acted as my bedside table. On the table stood a candle set in a saucer beside which lay a box of matches. A rickety chest of drawers completed the furnishings. A window with rusty hinges looked onto a neglected orchard. My new life as a farmer's boy had started. I was truly a boy in the mud.

The delicious smell of roast chicken wafted across the yard from the farm kitchen. Returning to the kitchen I saw that two places had been laid at the kitchen table. My mouth watered as roast chicken and potatoes were being dished up onto dinner plates. To my consternation, Mrs. Fordham carried them into the farmhouse dining room and I was left with the memory of the loaded plates and their inviting contents. A long time passed before Mrs. Fordham reappeared. Going to the larder, she selected a tin of war-time corned beef. "Help yourself, Michael" she said. "Tiny, our farm man, will be in soon and after you've both had lunch, he'll show you round the farm." Noticing my downcast expression, she added "Oh dear, you thought that the chicken was for you? I'm sorry; it was for our paying guests. They come down from London for a few days rest and quiet and to get away from the bombing and enjoy some good wholesome home coking."

While I hungrily made the best of my plate of corned beef, Tiny joined me at the table. He helped himself to the remainder of the meat. "That chicken smelt good!" He remarked with a grin.

Tiny was the tallest man I had ever seen. "Six foot four in my socks," he announced in his broad Irish brogue. He was to become my teacher and mentor during the six months that lay ahead.

Back in my room, I unpacked my suitcase and put on the working men's shirts, and heavy corduroy trousers which Moo had provided me. My boots fit well despite the extra thick woollen socks that she insisted that I wore in them. Feeling very new and far too clean, I ventured out onto the farm in search of Tiny.

The farm seemed dirty and untidy, but to me it was exciting to be beginning my life's work in the beautiful surroundings of a farm in Sussex. Farm life was all around me. I could see the cows out in the meadow and nearby a family of pigs were snoring contentedly as they enjoyed their afternoon siesta. There were some energetic Rhode Island Red hens scratching about in the straw and clucking as if in a state of gossip. And in a stable a sad looking horse scraped her hoof impatiently and awarded me with a friendly whinny and shake of her head.

Tiny was wheeling barrows of evil smelling manure up a steep plank to the top of a huge mound of muck that he called a midden. "Here you are, Michael." He said as he handed over the barrow already filled with straw and muck from the cowshed. "You can finish off this job for me."

The handles were filthy, and I could barely raise the legs of the barrow off the ground. Somehow I managed to reach the plank. Straining every muscle in my body, I launched myself and the barrow up the plank. Too soon, I lost my balance. My new boots sank deeply into the horrible smelly mire. The barrow tipped over and my hands and face were plunged into the morass. The new farm student had received his first lesson!

Water for the house and farm was pumped by hand from a well in the farm yard. This duty became my daily core. The pump was stiff and squeaky. Water would shoot out of the top and run inside my boot and soak my trousers. The water for the cows and the pigs had to be carried across to galvanized water troughs using a wooden yoke across my shoulders to which heavy buckets were attached. The yoke quickly made my shoulders sore. The daily routine of hard manual work had started. It was to become my way of life for the next twenty years.

The dairy cows were an assorted collection of quite mangy animals, descended from the old English Shorthorn breed. Milking times were at five o'clock every morning and four o'clock every afternoon. I had to learn how to milk by hand as milking machines had not as yet been invented. Prior to milking, the cowshed had to be mucked out. However, hygiene was not the farm's strong point. The milker's hands were often far from clean, and much dirt must have entered the milk. To me as a beginner this all seemed normal; little did I know how bad the farming and working conditions were. They were certainly not suitable for the training of a new recruit to the farming community.

My hard work was tempered by unexpected joys. I began to feel the benefit of the fresh air and the hard physical challenges which each day brought. Bedtime was always more than welcome. Tired and aching muscles were healed and restored by morning. Even the snorts and snores of the sow and her piglets who shared my shed did not keep me awake for long. Waking each morning, I would wash myself using a bucket of water from the well which was always icily cold.

There is a special feeling in the air just before dawn. For me, this is one of nature's great experiences. There is an air of mysticism, a deeply religious moment in time when the Creator is walking in his garden. A precious instant before humanity gets out and about to spoil the day and initiate a new morning of havoc and chaos.

Despite enjoying my work, I was intensely lonely and missed my family. They were now spread so widely apart from each other but I was consoled by a new friendship, with the cart horse. We got to know each other when Tiny suggested that I go to the stable to put on her harness.

The tack hung on a wall in the stable. The first item of harness was the large and heavy leather collar. I tried, and tried again, to get it over the mare's head but she stamped her foot and wagged her head in dismay. Tiny arrived. "The collar goes over her head upside down," he suggested kindly. "Then you can reverse it when it's on." My equine companion seemed to nod her head in approval.

Harnessing a working horse is quite easy when you know how, and I soon mastered the way in which it all fitted together in order to provide a powerful source of power. A draught horse could pull tremendous weights when correctly harnessed. The complete harness was known as the gear, and the whole unit of power created by horse and gear together amounted to 'one horse power'. This harness was in bad repair and I spent my spare time, as little as it was, repairing it with string and leather straps. These I stitched with a special harness needle.

This horse, so vital to the farm, did not appear to have a name. "I'll call you 'Haberdashery'," I said as I proudly led her out to work one morning. I soon shortened her name to Habba. Habba's vocabulary was small but essential. She reacted to 'Gee up' for starting, 'Whoa girl' for stopping and 'get back' for reversing. Steering was accomplished by gentle pressure on the bit in her mouth to the right or left as well as by use of the command 'Come round'.

Horses respond to positive and kind handling, and they love being praised. Habba's vocabulary soon increased to include 'Good girl', and on the occasions that she became stubborn, which was also one of Habba's few personality faults, she would be subjected to some basic rustic admonitions. I would go and say good night to her every evening. She never failed to console me and comfort me, for my loneliness often led to tears.

Summertime brought the vital, and in England's climate frustrating, season for making hay. Every available hand was recruited, even Elizabeth, the Fordham's daughter. She was a few years older than me and quite pretty. As I worked stripped to the waist in the hot sunshine, she game me inviting glances from time to time. She was away at boarding school most of the time which allowed us little time to get to know each other, but I felt the first awakening of an interest in the opposite sex. I had moved on by the time she returned after the autumn term.

The hay crop was heavy, and as rain was forecast, Mr. Fordham and Tiny decided to build a haystack at the lower end of the farm. As we worked the Royal Air Force was constructing an air strip in the valley adjoining the farm. We had nearly put the finishing touches to the apex roof of the stack, of which we were very proud, when an R.A.F. staff car sped across the fields towards us. A sergeant approached the boss aggressively. "I have orders to instruct you to remove that haystack at once" he announced.

"I'll not move it!" responded the irate farmer, "we're fighting a war against people like you, and we can't have little Hitlers here." The sergeant saluted smartly and sped away.

A few minutes later the car arrived back. This time the sergeant was accompanied by an officer. He approached Mr. Fordham apprehensively. "My Spitfires can't take off! Your haystacks are right at the end of the runway," he insisted politely. "You'll have to move it I'm afraid, but we'll help you transport it up to the farm if that would help." That afternoon and evening, with the help of the Royal Air Force air crew and ground staff, the stack was transported to a safe place near the farm yard. Next day we witnessed the first Spitfire taking off. We were honoured with a performance of the famous 'Victory Roll' traditionally given by fighter pilots when returning victorious from battle.

A letter from Moo, who wrote to me every week, announced that she intended to come down to visit me. I met her at the Bat and Ball and we made our way down the lane, which thankfully was now in its summer state of being dry and dusty. We were happy to be together again. Moo was pale and drawn though. The stress of living and working in London was very evident. I had become used to my room next to the pig sty. I was not prepared for her reaction when she saw it.

"Pack your bags," she insisted. "You're coming straight home with me." Moo wondered why I had not told her that I was being ill treated. She felt that the Fordham's were taking unfair advantage of me. Although I was much fitter, I was still very thin and ill nourished. I didn't want to give up and preferred to complete my six months as agreed with Mr. Fordham. I was determined to qualify for a place at the East Sussex School of Agriculture. Reluctantly Moo agreed to let me stay at Broad Oak Farm. She left without seeing Mr. or Mrs. Fordham. She was too angry. Her visit had unsettled me. I longed to return home with her, but my determination to remain independent and complete the course had triumphed.

Before long the six months were completed. Pops had arranged another interview! This time we went to Plumpton to meet with Mr. R.H.B. Jesse, Director of Agriculture and Principal of the East Sussex School of Agriculture. He was a dignified and kindly man, but on hearing about the conditions at Broad Oak Farm he became very concerned.

During the interview it became clear that we would be unable to meet the cost of my going to this school as a full time student. Mr. Jesse promised to help, and suggested that I might be able to attend the school as a 'working student'. I would attend classes, but work on the farm in the early morning, evening and week-ends in order to pay for my keep and training.

I returned to London for a few weeks. Upon arrival I slept almost non stop for two days. Moo was faced with the unpleasant task of washing my very smelly farm clothes. She discovered that I had been mending my socks with sticking plaster from a First Aid kit. She also concluded that I must have been washing my underwear in a muddy pond. The task before Moo was one which demanded all her ingenuity. My farm clothes wee consigned to the dust bin. To add to her workload, my sailor brother Eddie returned on leave from the Navy. He also had laundry needs. His uniform shirts and seaman's collars were also in need of washing!

As the days went by there was still no news from Mr. Jesse at Plumpton. One morning the letter arrived. I had been accepted to attend the East Sussex School of Agriculture in Plumpton as a working student. I would never forget my six months at Broad Oak Farm, the guidance and instruction that had come from Tiny or the companionship of Habba, but now I was on my way up the farming ladder. I heard much later that Broad Oak Farm had been taken over by the War Agricultural Committee under instruction from Mr. Jesse. War time powers provided opportunity for unproductive farmers to be removed and the land made to produce its full quota of food for the nation.

The Farming Ladder

The East Sussex School of Agriculture is situated in a beautiful position beneath the South Downs. The farm land includes a good variety of soil types, ranging from the upper greensand at the top of the downs, to the heavy, gault clay in the valley.

Another bus journey from Lewes took me through the lovely downland countryside. The nervousness, brought on by yet another new beginning, was overwhelming. I had been exhorted by Moo to try and overcome my excessive shyness. I found it difficult to look people in the face when talking to them. Little did I know that my life was on the verge of a complete transformation.

I arrived at the door of a farm cottage to be greeted in a loving and friendly way, by Mr. and Mrs. Alan Whistler. Alan was combining his job as a stockman, working with a dairy herd, with that of teaching the technical and practical skills at the farm school. They had given me a pleasant room all on my own. From the window I could see the majestic view of the Downs but the sounds I heard were most unusual. The noise of what sounded like a battle turned out to be coming from an area set aside for military training. Soldiers from Canada were training for the time when they would unite with the Allied forces and try to free the captive nations of Europe.

I was assigned to work with Tom in the Head Carter's department, which entailed, to my delight, working full time with the horses. My work was to pay for my way at school. My lodgings, food, and tuition would be covered by my work on the farm. Moo and Pops were able to give me a small amount of money to cover my costs during my limited amount of spare time. I had to work seven days a week during term time, but had a day off each week when the school was on holiday. The training that I had received from Tiny and Habba had yielded fruit. I was soon an integral part of the farm team. A horse called Captain was allotted to my care and together we spent many hard and happy hours at work on the farm. Our jobs included general farm work using a tumbrel, or two wheeled cart, which could be loaded and then tipped. I became skilled in placing loads of sand, manure, or feeding stuffs exactly in the right spot. Loads of manure were to be dropped in straight lines and equal distances apart. Then the manure was spread evenly over the ground by the men who followed us using four pronged forks with specially curved tines suitable for the job.

I must have trudged many miles behind Captain as he patiently pulled sets of harrows to work down the tilth of the fields in preparation for the sowing of the wheat, oats or barley. Much of the land on the sides of the South Downs was being ploughed for the first time in living memory and astonishingly large amounts of Charlock and indigenous weed appeared as their seeds, which had been dormant for perhaps a hundred years, germinated and created a vast carpet of yellow.

Captain was an intelligent animal. He had a mind of his own. He was an expert at pulling the horse-hoe exactly between the straight rows of roots or kale. He would make the job easy by keeping his place between the rows, without variation. When we came to the end of the rows, called the headlands in farming, he would execute a perfect turn and head down the next row as if he was programmed to do the job. However, he had a built in time clock and knew exactly the right time to stop for 'elevenses'. He would stop and have a short siesta, or munch some grass, while I enjoyed the flask of hot tea kindly provided for me by Mrs. Whistler. Captain became as good a friend as Habba had been.

Back in the stables it would be my job to help groom all the Shire cart horses after their hard days work. I would muck out the stables, then feed the horses and fill their racks with hay. There were about ten horses in all. They would often work in pairs and sometimes even in threes.

The first tractors were beginning to replace horse power on the farms. Fordson and John Deere tractors were arriving from the United States of America, lashed to the decks of the merchant ships. They arrived quite worse than new as a result of their sea voyage. They were the lucky ones. Many tractors ended up lying in the depths of the Atlantic Ocean since their merchant ships were bombed or torpedoed by the Germans. The war at sea was at its most savage stage and the toll of seamen's lives was very great.

Most days I was able to spend some time in my role as a farm student and the classroom work was enjoyable. Mr. Jesse taught botany and also crop rotations, the traditional methods of growing a variety of farm crops. I learned that the basis of all good husbandries was the succession of crops known as the Norfolk Rotation; wheat, roots, oats, barley, and then a year of rest, called the 'fallow'.

We even became familiar with the anatomy of the camel. Captain Farran had retired from the Veterinary Corps in the First World War. He had been pressed into service as our teacher of Veterinary Science. As he had spent much of his service years in Egypt, he used skeletons and diagrams of the camel to illustrate his lectures. Apparently the physiology of horse and camel are similar, although we used to remark that we had never met a horse that had a hump! We also began to be familiar with the workings of the internal combustion engine. We learned the back aching work of hand hoeing the root crops, and experienced the excitement and smothering dust created by the coming of the threshing machine.

As harvest time arrived, the sheaves of corn were stacked in the fields. The beautifully built corn stacks made up a picturesque landscape which has been lost from our countryside since the advent of the Combine Harvester. The sheaves were later fed into the noisy and fast revolving drum of the threshing machine. The corn was separated from the straw, the weeds, husks and cavings, or short pieces of straw. Sometimes the poor harvest mice were spewed out by the noisy and ingenious machine, which, in those days were still driven by a steam engine. The threshing gangs who operated these machines would travel from farm to farm.

The test of whether the young farm workers had reached manhood was taken at the time of threshing. The sacks of wheat weighed a massive two and a quarter hundredweight. You became a man on the day that you could carry a sack up a flight of wooden steps into the granary. I was toughening up. I could not manage this at first, but achieved success before the end of my year at Plumpton.

Other courses included the varied skills of pig and bee keeping. One day, the chief beekeeper took a group of us out for some practical experience of capturing a swarm of bees. The school had seven sets of protective clothing and nets, but there were eight students present. He called for a volunteer to manage without protection, whilst he himself had none. I was elected to be the volunteer. "Don't worry boy, they'll not touch you if you show no fear." He said. He proceeded to demonstrate the practice of puffing smoke at the bees in order to quiet them. The bees had other plans. I was immediately the subject of their attention. I could feel them crawling about in my hair. To the sound of the screams of laughter of my companions I took off in frenzy to find a water trough. Thankfully, I plunged my head into the water, which was none too clean. My head ached terribly. Safely back in the sick bay, the nurse bathed and dressed fourteen bee stings. She told me how lucky I was as it was believed that bee stings would give protection against rheumatism in later life. My hair, always untidy would have suited a scarecrow. Nurse had chopped it savagely with a blunt pair of scissors in order to carry out her act of first aid.

The Farm School undertook the initial training of girls who had joined the Women's Land Army. They were known as Land Girls. About twenty girls arrived every two weeks for a short introductory course in farm work. They learnt how to milk a cow, harness a horse, and do general farm and dairy duties. The arrival of each group of girls created excitement amongst the regular students who were all young men. The girls came from every walk of life and many from London and the suburbs. The Land girls were a very mixed bunch. Some were older women while others were in their teens. One morning I was transfixed in wonder by one of the new arrivals. I had never seen anyone as beautiful in my life. She was a London girl from East Ham.

Dorothy had never really experienced life in the country except for day excursions with her family as a child. She was terrified of all the animals. This was an awesome experience for her and she showed it. I longed to help her, to talk to her. Unfortunately, it took me the first week of her stay to overcome my shyness and to make friends with her. My opportunity came when it was my turn to teach her how to harness a horse. I used Captain as my model, and got great amusement watching her trying to overcome her fear and put the collar over his head.

My childhood and prior schooling had provided little contact with girls. Dorothy soon helped me to overcome all that. I was able to tell her about the way that I had learned to harness my friend Habba. I had never seen her laugh until then. We quickly made friends, and spent as much fee time as we could together. We had one blissful week of friendship. My gift of being able to play the piano came in useful. We discovered that the school's Assembly Hall was a quiet, unused area in the evening. We could sit side by side on the piano stool whilst I strummed the popular tunes of the day—'Smoke gets in your eyes', 'You'll never know just how much I love you' and another popular song of the time which told of 'two sleepy people, together in love, and too much in love to say goodnight'.

That's the way we were on the last night of her training course. We walked hand in hand for many miles that evening. But when we said a tearful goodbye, we were outside the front door of the school. Here Dorothy shared her dormitory accommodations. She suddenly hugged me and gave me a gentle kiss. I had been too shy to take the initiative! I crept back to my room. The Whistlers, realizing that I was experiencing my first love, had tactfully left the back door of the cottage unlocked. I ended up with a sleepless but thoughtful night.

I never saw Dorothy again. She left the next morning to start work on a farm to which she had been assigned. We exchanged letters for a month or so and hoped to meet in Lewes. But we could never manage to arrange our time off together. Suddenly, her letters were discontinued. I had no more news of Dorothy until some years later I heard from a friend that she had met a Canadian soldier in a pub near the farm where she worked. He had obviously not been slow to respond to her beauty and personality.

Goatlake Farm and The Traveller's Rest

A local Public House features in my memory for each of the family homes of my childhood. We were a pub going family. Moo and Pops made the most of their contacts in the 'local' to which they always attached themselves. In one of these homes from home Moo heard about the Beresford's. Mr. Beresford had owned a Motor Garage somewhere in the Kensington area of London. He and his wife had decided to escape the blitz and buy a small farm in Devon but Mr. Beresford knew little about farming. The Beresford's needed a young man to work on their farm as a personal assistant.

The pub fraternity was following the ongoing drama of Roy and Dorothy Bishop's son, the farm boy, with interest. They all decided that I was just the boy to send down to Devonshire to assist the Beresford's. The thought of moving to a farm in Devonshire, where I thought I would be able to put my new found training to good use, was very exciting. So off I went to Goatlake Farm for my next adventure.

The farm was small and its land was derelict and totally disorganized. There were a few South Ham cows and some mangy looking sheep. A bad tempered cart horse called Polly was the only 'powered' unit. She was used to pull the very limited amount of farm equipment.

There are many stories which could be told from this disastrous appointment. However my thoughts turn to two pubs, the Red Lion Inn in the village of Dunsford and The Traveller's Rest situated on the road from Exeter to Okehampton. The Beresfords were what the Devonshire farming community would refer to as townies. Life for me was very lonely because there were no other young people of my age in the area, and since I was always hungry where better to go in my time of need than to the local public houses.

One evening Mr. Jack Smallridge, the village blacksmith, to whom I had taken Polly for a new pair of shoes, invited me to join him for a drink at the Red Lion. The Red Lion was a typical village pub of the time. Located in a pretty village in the Teign Valley, it proved to be a friendly tavern. There were few comforts inside but this was a popular meeting place for the men of the village. Much fun and laughter was shared as they amused themselves playing games of dominoes, table skittles, or gambling over a pack of cards.

Country people love to share a joke and a new young fellow fresh from an agricultural school in Sussex was fair game for a bit of leg pulling and ribaldry. Young Michael had to be initiated into the wonders of scrumpy drinking. Scrumpy, or rough cider, was brewed in the barns of local farmers, notable Roger Grey and Reg Moore. Now if you have never experienced that specialty beverage of Devonshire perhaps you should try it some day! But be very careful since the alcohol content is very high. Needless to say, I was quickly plied with several pints of scrumpy and a delicious pasty or two. My shyness, which was always a great problem to me, evaporated as I joined in the local songs and played a game or two of dominoes. More pints of scrumpy cider kept appearing before me. "Drink up, Mike!" Jack insisted and another pint was on its way down into my already overloaded stomach.

"Time Gentlemen, please," the landlord called using the traditional shout to notify his customers that closing time was in fifteen minutes. I tried to rise to my feet. I felt as if I had lost the use of my knees and was unable to get to my feet. To the amusement and cheers of all, I was grabbed by strong hands and hauled on to my feet. I was thrust outside into the fresh night air.

Seated on a wooden bench outside the Red Lion, I slowly regained control of my legs. It was a long time before I was able to balance sufficiently in order to mount and ride my bicycle. A shortcut home by way of a narrow footpath took me across a small meadow. I man-handled my bike over a high stile and peddled erratically heading for the lights of the farmhouse. There was little night illumination and the sky was very dark. Suddenly my front wheel struck something large yet rather soft. There was a horrifying squeal and I was launched forward over the bike's handle bars. An enormous sow which had been asleep on the footpath sped away into the darkness. A frightened, wretched, drunken and bruised young man eventually crept into the farmhouse and crawled into his bed. I was soon sound asleep! Despite this experience the Red Lion became a pleasant port of call. My lesson had been learned and I was now fully aware of the alcoholic content and dangers of over indulging in Devonshire scrumpy.

I declined the meagre breakfast that awaited me next morning. Mrs. Beresford was so concerned about me that she intended calling the doctor. I was compelled to confess my experience of the previous evening. The Beresfords were not amused but said little about it. They then ignored me for the remainder of the day. However, a good day's work soon revived my spirits.

My only personal transportation was my bicycle. On one occasion I made an attempt to ride Polly, the cart horse, to the pub. My expedition ended in a painful bruise to my shoulder. Polly purposely trotted under an overhanging branch of a tree. I was knocked to the ground and then struggled to my feet as my mischievous mount pawed the ground and blew down her nostrils as if to say, "I'm a cart horse, that's what you get for treating me like a hunter."

I loved the countryside and my chosen life as a farm boy, but I also enjoyed the very few occasions when I would have the day off. On these days I would often make my way to the County of Devon's capital city, Exeter. I would wander into the Cathedral Close at Exeter and venture inside that ancient and beautiful building. The Cathedral was damaged as a result of a bomb that fell during an air raid on Exeter. The city had been targeted in a series of German air attacks which became known as the Baedeker raids. Fortunately Exeter did not suffer the safe fate as Coventry, in the English midlands. That city was devastated by a vicious attack that fully destroyed the Cathedral. Many people thought that Hitler's Luftwaffe pilots were using Baedeker, the tourist guide book of the period, in order to locate and select their targets!

The quietness of the Cathedral, the echo of the sound of a chair being moved, the distant murmur of prayers being said, and the best of all, the great organ being played, thrilled me. I would take high tea in Tinleys, a small café in Cathedral Close, in Exeter. Rationing regulations decreed that one was only allowed to spend a few shillings on a meal in a café or restaurant. I would indulge in the luxury of a poached egg on toast.

On one such evening, I decided to call in at The Traveller's Rest, a small country pub that lay on my way home. I opened the door apprehensively. Inside I saw a cosy and pleasant bar which ran almost the full length of the house. Behind the bar a large man stood with a beaming, welcoming smile. "Come on in old chap" he greeted me. "What's it going to be? Scrumpy?" I declined. "Half of bitter then," he conceded.

Little did I know that I was talking to Jack Spurway, the man who would one day become my father-in-law. My friendship with Jack and Audrey Spurway, proprietors of The Traveller's Rest in Whitestone, near Tedburn St. Mary, Devon, was motivated by the fact that their pub kitchen produced the tastiest Cornish pasties in the neighbourhood.

Their pub was what is known as a 'Free House'. This means that the proprietor is free to buy beer from any brewery. Other pubs are often owned by a local brewery and are restricted to serving the beers made by their owners. I had learned to love the characters that frequented the bars of England's pubs. The company at The Traveller's Rest was typically varied. The locals, from the farms and villages nearby, mingled with travellers who dropped in for a break from their journeys between the charming city of Exeter and the busy market town of Okehampton.

The pub was also a favourite refuge for the soldiers, sailors and airmen of the allied armed forces. Jack and Audrey gave them a very cheerful welcome. The Traveller's Rest was a home away from home for all of us. Jack himself had once been a 'Mountie'. His experience in the Royal Canadian Mounted Police was put into good use as he served the rather high spirits of his military customers. He also once served as a police sergeant in the local constabulary. His truncheon hung behind the bar where everybody could clearly see it. With such volatile young men, and their girlfriends, present on any evening, tensions and tempers could quickly arise. Jack would often be seen standing tall at his full height of six foot four inches, twirling his truncheon. "There won't be any trouble, gentlemen, will there?" he would boom. He also made it known that he had a good relationship with the Military Police. Seldom did any hot blooded Canadian or American, or for that matter Pole, Frenchman, or Briton over step the mark.

Although the evenings were boisterous, the pub was a restful place during the working day and especially quiet during the midday period. One day I had arrived on my bike and instead of placing my usual half pint of beer and a pasty on the counter, Jack said, "You look as if you could do with a good square meal, Mike. We're just about to have lunch, why not come out into the back and have your meal with us." The aroma of good food seeping through to the bar was irresistible. I readily accepted his invitation.

Thereafter, my visit to the pub frequently included lunch with the landlord and his wife. I was made to feel like one of the family. On one such visit, Audrey announced that there would be an extra person for lunch the following weekend. "Our daughter, Valerie, will be home from school next week," she explained. I protested that, in that case, I would leave them to enjoy their daughter's visit. Privately, I saw the presence of an as yet unknown school girl as quite a threat. I felt insecure and apprehensive that my safe haven at the Traveller's Rest was to be invaded.

When the following Saturday arrived I decided the chance of having an excellent lunch at The Traveller's Rest was too good to miss. I convinced myself that I need not take much notice of the schoolgirl daughter so I made my way into the pub.

What I saw was a tall, attractive and athletic looking girl. When I was introduced to Valerie we shook hands and proceeded to make rather formal and polite conversation. We quickly discovered that we both have a love for animals. I was introduced to her pet dogs and she took me out to the stable where I met her pony. In the rear of the pub, a shed was occupied by a family of pigs. They were clearly intoxicated as they were being fed the dregs of the beer barrels. We laughed together as they rolled drunkenly across to the feeding trough to greet us.

After meeting the animals, lunch was excellent as usual. The meeting that I had dreaded had turned out to be more enjoyable than I could have imagined. We agreed to meet again the following week.

The days soon passed. Rather than staying at the pub, we went into Exeter by bus. Here we walked through the Close and into the Cathedral. The tranquillity within the ancient building held us entranced. Afterwards we made our way to Tinley's for tea. Over tea we tried to control our tendency to collapse into giggles. Mirth was generated by everything that was happening around us. We shared our stories of school, life on the farm and family.

Valerie told me how she had been confirmed as a member of the Church of England in the Cathedral. It had been, she said, a wonderful day in her life. I reflected that I too had once been confirmed but that my experience had not led me to become a churchgoer. As I made my way home that evening, I reflected that I enjoyed our conversation. I also wondered that perhaps I should follow up on my own membership of the Church some day. Pedalling back to the farm I felt that despite my anxieties about going into town with my new friend, the day turned out not to be so bad after all.

My days at Goatlake Farm were of little significance from a farming point of view. I gained a little additional experience and made new friends. The Spurway family had become good and supportive friends and my friendship with Valerie was a happy and warm experience. We liked one another, but would not at that point ever imagine that we were destined to fall in love and marry. I learned later the 'Lodgie', the lady who cooked the delicious meals at the pub, predicted that we would marry one day!

One Saturday, I chose to celebrate my birthday at the pub. Jack had greeted me with the usual glass of beer. As I lifted it up to acknowledge his wishes for a happy birthday, I looked at Jack and said, "I have something to tell you Mr. Spurway. This is the first legal pint of beer that I have consumed in your pub."

Jack's eyes twinkled kindly as he responded, "You don't think that I didn't know that, do you Mike?" He then added, "Here, have it on the house." In fact, the drinks were 'on the house' for all those present.

Now that my birthday had passed, I began to think more about my future. The Goatlake Farm rung of the farming ladder was at best creaky and not destined to be a foothold from which to climb higher. I felt the need to contact Mr. Jesse, Principal of the East Sussex School of Agriculture for advice so I wrote a letter to him. He had promised all his students that he would always be ready to help them if at any time they felt he could be of assistance. My letter ended up with the Chailey and District Agricultural Committee. From here I was given an introduction to a Mr. Thurston Matthews, a farmer from Staffordshire who was known as one of the best farmers in Sussex. He farmed Ockley Manor Farm, near Hassock in East Sussex, and there was a vacancy for a young man to assist him on the farm.

Farmer Roger Evans and his wife, whose farm was adjacent to Goatlake Farm, had become a good friend and confidante during my time there. On hearing the news about this new opportunity to move to Sussex, he insisted that I leave immediately, giving a minimum of notice to the Beresfords. "You don't owe them anything, Michael." He insisted, "Grab this chance to escape from a dead end situation."

The escape plans were made. He would come to Goatlake Farm with his farm truck and pick me up in two days time. From there he would take me to Exeter Station to catch the London train. I felt guilty in making such a hasty departure from Goatlake Farm. Jack and Audrey Spurway agreed with Roger's advice and added their encouragement to help me make the decision. Having loaded my suitcase and bicycle into the back of his truck, we made our way to Exeter. On the way we called in at the Traveller's Rest for a farewell pint of beer. I wondered if I would ever see them all again. The Traveller's Rest had become a real 'home from home'. I parted from them that day with a sad heart.

The Great Western Railway steam train which pulled into Exeter Station heralded a great change in my life. Valerie and I had agreed to keep in touch. I would be back in my beloved adoptive County of East Sussex but a long way from my new friends in Devonshire.

The War Ends With Sadness

Ockley Manor Farm was farmed to perfection. The contrast with Goatlake Farm was unbelievable. Thurston Matthews had been reared and brought up on the family farm in the County of Staffordshire. He was a tough and gruff personality, but his farming was renowned as being of the very best. He was to prove to be a hard taskmaster but an excellent roll model and teacher.

I hadn't been challenged by the tasks assigned to me at Goatlake Farm. I had not been subject to discipline and although I worked very hard and kept long hours, I had been virtually my own boss.

The first lesson to be learned at Ockley Manor Farm was that of strict time keeping. My job was to arrive at the cowsheds, which housed a large pedigree herd of Ayrshire cows, at 5 a.m. every morning. The stalls were to be mucked out and washed down in preparation for the arrival of Mr. Matthews and the rest of the staff at 5:30 a.m. The boss supervised the thorough preparation of the animals for the machine milking. The cows' udders were to be washed in warm water just prior to the moment when the milking machine clusters were attached. Each animal would then let down her milk so that the milking time would be quick and efficient. Mr. Matthews gave the commands and I carried them out. Sometimes the cows were cooperative but at other times they were neurotic. When I completed the early shift I would go back to my lodgings for a delicious breakfast prepared for me by Mrs. Weekes.

"So y'er with the wider woman," one of the men remarked on the first morning. Mrs. Weekes was known as the widow woman. She was allowed to live in the farm cottage rent free in return for providing food and lodging for the young farm boys. I was fortunate to be the only young man in her charge for most of my time at Ockley Manor Farm and she cared for me well. Despite war time rationing a huge breakfast was always ready on the table when I returned from my early morning duties.

Mrs. Weekes would greet me with a kindly exhortation. "Now get your hands washed Michael, and get tucked in to your breakfast." I could not linger over breakfast. I was expected back in the farm yard by 8 o'clock. Thurston Matthews would be waiting on the concrete apron with his pocket watch in hand. I was late on only one occasion.

"I'd 'ave been ashamed of mesel' if I'd 'ave bin late for work when I was your age," commented the boss. It was not said in anger, but quietly and thoughtfully. This stern, but fair man quickly won my affection and admiration and laid the foundation for the life of hard work and long hours that was just beginning in earnest.

The long winter evenings in the company of widow Weekes proved to be quite an adventure. She would spend much of her time sitting in her large armchair knitting or darning my socks. The love of her life was a black Cocker Spaniel whose name was Spider.

Spider was quite a character and would settle down on the second armchair beside the splendid log fire. I was not as fortunate as the dog. I was only given the use of one of the kitchen chairs! Mrs. Weekes would go out one evening a week. On these occasions I would relax in her chair by the fire. Spider would look across at me from his privileged position with a soulful expression as if demanding 'what are you sitting in *her* chair for?'

Some weeks later I discovered where Mrs. Weekes went for her evening out. One day Fred Chambers, one of the farm workers, informed me rather solemnly that 'wider Weekes' was a medium. "She's a spiritualist, Michael," he said. I wondered what a spiritualist was. "She gets in touch with the dead," Fred enlightened me. "Talks to 'em by all accounts," Fred's face became even more mournful. "Talks to 'er dead 'usband, so they say."

I became uneasy on those dark nights when he wind howled around the little cottage. I would imagine that I heard footsteps when the timbers creaked. I would bury my head beneath the bedclothes and wish that I was safely back at home in Pops' and Moo's flat in London. My mind was in turmoil. Did ghosts really exist? Did people go to heaven when they died? Was it possible for them to become stranded between heaven and earth letting them re-visit their home and loved ones? Could Mrs. Weekes really get in touch with her dead husband? Was he, perhaps, in the house now?

Some evenings later I had an experience which literally made my hair tingle and feel as if it was standing on end. We had finished one of Mrs. Weekes' tasty high teas. The fire glowed cheerfully in the grate and I was drowsy and just about to go up to bed. Suddenly the door of the sitting room blew open. Spider jumped down from his chair and moved towards the door, his head up looking as if he could see someone there and his tail wagging vigorously. Mrs. Weekes looked at me and said very quietly, "Don't be alarmed, Michael. It's Mr. Weekes." Spider came back across the floor and instead of jumping on his chair, lay down beneath it contentedly, his head on the floor and his tail still wagging slowly.

I waited, frozen with fear for a time. I can't recall how long a period it was. Then I said, "It's been a hard day. I think I'll go up to bed." I wasn't sure if I should give the presence of Mr. Weekes a friendly nod so I gave Mrs. Weekes a timid grin, bend down and patted Spider's head, and fled up the stairs. Back in the safety of my room, questions began racing into my mind. Had this really been the spirit of Mr. Weekes, or had I merely experienced a strong gust of wind and let my imagination run wild. I kept my experience to myself and preferred to believe that Mrs. Weekes was probably balmy and maybe Spider was a spiritualist too!

Time sped by at Ockley Manor Farm. The experience that I gained in dairy and general farming, coupled with the exhilaration of hard manual work day by day caused me to grow both physically and in my knowledge of farming and the world. The men that I worked alongside day by day provided my education. They were the dearest and gentlest of companions. They had only the benefit of a basic education in the village schools but were very sharp indeed at solving problems of all kinds. In my turn at this farm, I was privileged to be educated by them. The training that I received at Ockley Manor Farm certainly moved me to a secure and valuable rung higher up the farming ladder.

During the latter days of my sojourn at Ockley Manor Farm the saddest event of my life took place. My brother Edward was away serving in the Navy in the Far East, and Moo and Pops had moved into in a first floor flat in Ladbroke Grove, Nottinghill Gate in London. I was called back to London. Pops, it seemed, was critically ill having suffered a severe brain haemorrhage. I hurried to London to find Moo in deep distress and Pops unconscious. There was little that could be done. It was May 5, 1945, my brother's birthday, wherever he was. The war was close to its end.

I went into see Pops lying rather restlessly in his bed. As I bent over him I said, "It's all over Pops, the war has ended." I shall never know if I imagined it or not for there had been no communication with him for the past twenty four hours, but I thought he gave me a smile. A few hours later he died. Moo and I were on our own now. We would have to make our own way through life.

Captain Roy Bishop almost survived the second war in his lifetime, only just missing "Victory in Europe Day". Here in London, at home from the war, my father died on May 5, 1945, just before Winston Churchill's announcement that the war was over. He was only 49 years old. His life was too short. It was stress and hypothermia which brought about his death. The Second Great War had finally claimed him.

Shortly after his death, Moo and I heard that Londoners were making their way to Buckingham Palace. The King and Queen were to appear on the famous balcony of the palace. "We must go," Moo announced. "Roy would have wanted to take you down there." Putting on her hat and coat, off we went. This was an experience never to be forgotten. People who were complete strangers were hugging and kissing each other. There was dancing in the streets. A solid wedge of Londoners was moving down The Mall towards the great meeting place. We managed to reach the very railings of the Palace. The Royal Family appeared on the balcony. Then Winston Churchill, our great war time Prime Minister, stepped onto the balcony, cigar in mouth, hat in hand. The acclamation of the crowd was deafening. We wept and laughed together. "How your father would have loved to be here," Moo said. If it is possible that the dead can visit us, or be near us, I thought perhaps he was.

His funeral took place on "Victory in Europe Day". The hearse and our accompanying car drove through London where people were dancing in the streets. Huge bonfires were being lit as timber was pulled out from the bombed out houses. Pop's coffin was draped with the Union Jack and as we passed by many soldiers and sailors, seeing the procession, doffed their caps, stood to attention and saluted. An unknown warrior was passing by. He had served his country in the past. Now the future was theirs. As the Remembrance Day service has so aptly proclaimed ever since of those who died either during the war or from war's mental and physical wounds, *They shall grow not old as we who are left grow old; nor shall the years condemn. At the going down of the sun, and in the morning we shall remember them*.

My happiest memories of Pops are from the pre-war period. I still recall vividly Pops sitting at his typewriter, set up on a table in the large garden of Sturdie House in the shade of the cedar tree, and then later in our home in Sussex, with Squashy, his faithful terrier at his feet, and my mother busy in the house and garden.

Pops recorded many of his war time thoughts in the form of poetry. One which we found scribbled in his military notebook many years later read, *'Whether my life is long or short greatly depends on Viscount Gort, or, on the steadiness of hand of some exuberant Allemand.'* Many years later I discovered a poem that he had written. The poem was titled *'After'* and read:

When death comes, let it be with strain
Of sweetest music to my brain.
If death be sleep—then let me be
Content with immortality.
If death be life, then I shall reap
The dear benefits of sleep—
But this I know, if death be love
Always I wait for you above.

His Lordship's Cows and Pigs

With such significant changes occurring in my life and in the world, I determined that it was time to move onward and upward again. This time the East Sussex School of Agriculture recommended that I snatch up an opportunity to work under a young Danish farmer who had recently become Farm Manager of Buckhurst Farm in Withyham, near Hartfield in east Sussex. Buckhurst Farm was the home estate of Lord and Lady De La Warr. Now based at this attractive estate, Lord De La Warr, who had served in Churchill's wartime cabinet as Postmaster General, was a country farmer. He took great pride in his herd of pedigree Jersey cows and his pedigree Wessex Saddleback pigs.

Arnold Christensen, the young Danish Farm Manager, and his family occupied the Farm Manager's house. I would live in the farmhouse 'as family' with his wife and baby daughter, who were both delightful. I had been fortunate to be chosen to work under his direction since Mr. Christensen was already well known as a leading and skilful farm manager. I was thrilled to be on a Sussex farm which was held out as the most progressive and excellently managed in the county.

My work at Buckhurst was divided between the care of Jersey cows and the Wessex Saddleback pigs. The care of this valuable herd of cows was first class. The pedigree bulls were lordly and the cows, though not always ladylike, were beautiful. The milk produced was of the highest quality and the attention they received by way of diet and veterinary supervision was superior to that afforded many of the ordinary citizens of the land.

One cow, Buckhurst Magic, was the queen of the herd. She was to become the centre of my life. I was assigned as her personal care provider and I was supervised by John the head herdsman. One day we proudly loaded Magic into a cattle truck and made our way up to London to attend the National Dairy Show at the great Exhibition Centre in Olympia.

The occasion was memorable as we carefully unloaded our precious cargo. We led her along the rows of the other elegant showgirls which had already arrived from the best British dairy farms. Each cow had been allotted their own stall. Dwarfed by the other breeds in size, the little Jerseys were the debutantes from the noble farms of Britain. Bottles of shampoo were quickly put into use, tails were being combed, backs trimmed and udders tenderly examined in case any accidental bruises had been caused by the journey. It was a scene of quiet excitement and professional business.

Magic became the focus of attention and held court to a great many visitors on her first evening. I was just wondering what arrangements had been made for the night when John, the herdsman, announced casually over a cup of tea from his thermos flask that we would have to take it in turns to guard Magic by both day and night. My duty would be to guard her and to sleep beside her. The Dairy show, he explained, is a dangerous place. Stable boys had to guard their famous race horses, check their food and examine their water in order to avoid enemy attempts to knobble them before a great race. So then would we, as champion dairy cows were liable to be subject to the wiles of competitive herdsmen. In the event that one's cow was considered to have a chance of taking home the championship, you would have to be extremely alert. One of dastardly tricks known to be played by malicious competitors was to sneak in and milk out one of their challenger's four quarters, thus making her udder lopsided and unattractive. We kept a vigilant eye on all doubtful looking herdsmen or women who ventured nearby. No one must ever be allowed to touch her!

His Lordship was determined to win the championship with Magic. We did all that we could to make Buckhurst Magic comfortable, and bedded her down for the night. The show cows would have one day in which to adjust to their new surroundings before the judging took place.

I left John on guard while I went to telephone my mother to say that I would not be able to come to have a meal with her, let alone stay the night as planned. I would be spending the night with Magic as her guard!

As night fell, Olympia closed and all the visitors left the exhibition hall. I realised that I was in the midst of an unusual and exciting experience. I could hear the rattle of the neck chains as the cattle settled uneasily into their temporary London quarters. Watchful eyes were cast upon strangers as they passed by the stalls. In the air there was a buzz of conversation as herdsman renewed old friendships and swapped their stories. Laughter punctuated the air as jokes were shared and calming words of reassurance could be heard being given to the very important cows in their charge. The varied accents demonstrated that those in attendance had assembled from farms right across the length and breadth of the nation. Together, this created a remarkable atmosphere which combined apparent friendship with the high spirit of competition. At length the time came for the dimming of the lights. Here we were in the centre of London but the farm-yard smell and the soft lowing of the cattle made it difficult to believe

John shared the keeping of the night watch. We would take turns of four hours on duty, followed by four hours of rest and an uneasy sleep. I snuggled up against Magic's warm back with a Hessian sack stuffed with straw for a pillow.

On the day of the championship competition, I awoke at five in the morning. John was already at work preparing Magic for her momentous day. The quietness of the night soon abated and a busy scene emerged as the cattle lines were cleaned and fresh straw was laid. Next the proud owners began to arrive. Lord De La Warr, known to us affectionately as 'Lordy', and Lady De La Warr arrived and paid homage to Magic, who by now was prepared for the starting of the competition. She revelled in the adulation afforded to her and seemed to sense her own importance.

Our hopes were high. We had been unable to identify any other Jersey cow that was, in our opinion, so lovely as Magic. Her temperament and personality were considered to be a strong factor in her favour.

A bell was rung and an announcement asked all those with Jersey cows to make their way to the judging ring. Donned in a spotless white coat, I proudly walked Magic into the ring. Here I fell under the eyes of the expert, knowledge-able, but inscrutable men and women who were judging the entries. We paraded around the arena. Magic never so much as disgraced herself by indiscreetly soiling the fresh new sawdust on which she walked. She picked her way daintily around the ring like a ballerina.

Our excitement rose to fever pitch as we were signalled to parade around the ring a second time. Already other less beautiful cows were being politely ushered back to their stalls. The short list reduced the competition to just four prima donnas. One more was escorted out of the ring of champions. Three were left. One more was beckoned to, but this one was signalled to take up her place in the centre of the ring.

The remaining two finalists were signalled to make yet another circuit of the ring. The judge came across to Magic. An attendant hovering nearby was holding a large red rosette. He came across to Magic and pinned it on to her halter. Magic had just been crowned the Queen of all Jersey cows!

The crowd burst into loud applause. Lordy entered the ring to share in our moment of glory. The head herdsman John, after receiving the congratulations of the proud breeder and owner, led our champion on a lap of honour.

My next assignment at Buckhurst Farm was to assist Mr. Smith. Smith, as he insisted on being called, managed and nursed the Wessex Saddleback pigs with just as much care as John lavished on Magic. The piggery was noisy and a more smelly place in which to work. Although I was surprised to observe that pigs are cleaner in their habits than cows, always choosing the same corner of their pen in which to go to the toilet.

If Magic was famous, so were her neighbours. The Buckhurst herd of pedigree Wessex Saddleback pigs were comprised of aristocratic piggy ladies and gentlemen of similar fame and grandeur. They totalled more than five hundred in number. Smith was a dour and silent character. He carried the aroma of his trade with him. I, too, soon acquired the same pervasive odour as I became immersed in the day to day activities amongst his Lordship's pigs.

Every new piglet had its weight recorded at birth and at weekly intervals. Each animal had its own identity tag clipped into its ear, an operation which I felt, at first, was cruel. The tagging involved a quick squeeze of the ear marking stapler, a hideous shriek, a flap of the large black ears, and then proud acceptance of having been adopted as part of Lordy's farming family. After all that they seemed to be proud to be his Lordship's pigs.

The aftermath of the war meant that farm foodstuffs were still in short supply. Household scraps of waste food, known as swill, were collected from the big house, farm cottages, and the villages. These food scraps were then boiled in large caldrons and mixed with crushed cereals. This was exhausting work as the mass of stinking food was turned by hard labour using long handled shovels. When ready for feeding to the animals, the texture was like that of a huge mass of porridge.

The noise of five hundred aristocratic pigs of all ages screaming with anticipation of the arrival of their main meal has to be heard to be believed. We would often demonstrate to visitors that total silence could be achieved. It was one of our pig parlour tricks. At the blowing of a loud and shrill whistle, the whole family of pigs would become still and silent for about three seconds. After a short interval the cacophony would resume. When feeding time was completed, the sound of contented slurping would soon be followed by a chorus of happy snoring Saddlebacks settling down for their siesta.

The aroma of the piggery was duly noted on the occasions of my free weekends. Farm hands worked long hours for very little reward. I was allowed just one weekend off each month when I would visit my mother's flat in Battersea, London. I had little opportunity for social activities, but the smell of the Buckhurst piggery was not lost on the landlord and customers of the pub at the corner of Park Gate Street. "Mikes back from looking after his Lordship's pigs." Moo would announce with great pride.

Some wag would inevitably quip in response, "And when's he going back!"

Back at Buckhurst, I became an experienced baby sitter for the Christensen's. I could usually manage to dispel fits of crying by their baby daughter by telling stories about Magic or the naughty and noisy piggies. This was a happy period in my life, but before I had time to put down roots, a new adventure and opportunity was presented to me. I was invited to take part in an exchange of farm students. The next rung on the farming ladder would take me to Denmark.

Danish Bacon

I was to take part in an exchange of farm students organized by the National Farmer's Union and it's counterpart in Denmark. Danish farming was held in high regard in England, especially their production of bacon and butter. If I was to qualify for a position as Farm Bailiff or Manager in the future, it would be important to have experienced life and work on a Danish farm. Arnold Christensen had secured a place for me on a farm owned by the Justesen Brothers, proprietors of a Danish brewery. They owned a farm at Viby, near Roskilde, on the Island of Sjælland.

My journey to Denmark began in Harwich, where I boarded my ferry. Before long we were at sea. The ship pitched and rolled its way through the turbulent North Sea. There was an unpleasant smell of sea sickness as the Danish ferry ploughed a straight furrow across to Esbjerg. The journey heightened my anxiety, and prompted the question, "What on earth are you doing here?" But I was confident that I was in the right place at the right time.

On an earlier occasion I had considered a similar change; though at that time I considered immigrating to Canada. Young men could get an assured job on a farm in Canada and a sea passage for just £10 in the immediate post war period. On that occasion I stood in a long line of young farm workers who had also decided to head for Canada. I had paid for my ten pounds and was in line for the compulsory immunization injections when suddenly the full realization of what I was doing came into my mind. My brother Eddie was serving overseas with the Navy, Pops was dead, and dear Moo, I suddenly realised, would be completely alone if I went away to Canada.

My mind was in turmoil. There were now just ten men ahead of me, one of whom was a burly and tough looking man. He proceeded to faint at the sight of a nurse administering the needle in the arm of a rather weedy fellow, who seemed not to have felt the prick at all. I pulled out of line. The men in the line behind jeered and mocked me. "Coward!" They shouted. One spoke the truth without realizing it when he taunted, "Want to go home to Mummy then?"

One of my problems at that age was the tendency to blush. My face would immediately betray my feelings when embarrassed. I fled from the immigration department's barrack-like centre forgetting to reclaim my ten pounds, a month's wages for me at the time, and raced home to find Moo. She had clearly been crying. She looked at me in astonishment. "It's alright," I said. "I'm not going." At that time, I immediately knew that I had made the right decision. My exchange to Denmark, however, would only take me away from England for only a few months.

With the journey by ferry complete, I bought a rail ticket to Roskilde, the ancient city in which the Kings and Queens of Denmark are buried within the walls of the famous Domkirke. My ride across Denmark by train gave me my first experience of foreign travel. The international use of English was not so usual in those days and I had to use my wits to find my way. Even buying Danish sandwiches was a challenge! I was on my own in a foreign land.

On arrival in Roskilde I was met by Herr Hansen, Farm Manager at Scousbo Avlsgaard. This was the farm on which I would work for the next three months. Herr Hansen greeted me kindly and led me out of the station carrying my bulky suitcase. I expected to see a car, van, or perhaps some kind of farm truck, but by using sign language he indicated that I should climb onto the pillion seat of his motor bike. He balanced my suitcase precariously across the bike's handlebars. I was no sooner aboard, with hardly any time to grasp him firmly around his waist, before he moved off. We careened down the main highway at an alarming pace. I had never ridden pillion on a motorcycle before and I was terrified. Soon Herr Hansen turned off the main road. Without slackening his speed he made his way down a gravel track for several miles before arriving safely, yet shaken, at Scousbo.

My new home was a pleasant house beside a small lake. This was the hostel in which the young farmhands lodged. Herr Hansen showed me to a small bedroom. The room was simply, but pleasantly, furnished. It was quite the cosiest and nicest room I had ever had. The bed was adorned with a comfy duvet. I had not seen this form of bedding before. I was soon to discover the warmth and comfort of a Scandinavian bedroom.

Lunch time arrived and the farm hands were assembling around the traditional long dining table in the farmhouse. Everyone remained standing until Herr Hansen took his seat at the head of the table. I was the centre of intense interest from the villainous looking group of young men with whom I was to live and work.

The spectacle of young men with shoulder length hair had not at that time been seen in England, yet two fellows, to whom I immediately attributed my own label as 'the Vikings', wore their blond hair at shoulder length. The young men of the farm turned out to be far friendlier than their villainous looks had suggested. A burly young man with a friendly and welcoming grin came across, and speaking in Danish bid me welcome. He was blond too, but wore his hair short and smartly clipped. Then there was Thorkild Holm, the farm's Foreman, who was to become a much valued friend and helper.

At work I wore a maroon coloured beret like the ones worn by the British Commando Regiment and made famous by Field Marshal Lord Montgomery of El Alamein. Denmark had spent the war years as an occupied county. The war was still very much in the minds of her people. They had suffered grievously at the hands of the German invaders and after their liberation General Montgomery had become their hero. He had visited Denmark wearing his famous beret. I was the first Englishman that these country men had met so my new companions immediately conferred their own nickname upon me. I became known in the locality as 'Monty, the Englander'.

As I had arrived in the late spring, my time on the farm was largely filled with the exhausting task of singling the long straight rows of emerging sugar beet plants. My companions were using a short handled hand hoe. The young Danes could undertake this task at a slow walking pace suing a deft and accurate twist of their wrists. This would accomplish a near perfect result leaving just one strong plant at regular intervals along the seemingly never ending rows. I was left far behind as I struggled to gain the skills needed to do the job efficiently. As they disappeared into the distance they would taunt me, trying out the English I was beginning to teach them. "Come on, poor old Englander!"

Later Thorkild took pity on me and introduced me to the huge Percheron work horses used by the farm. The age of tractors was only just beginning to dawn on the farmhands of Denmark. I was put to work horse hoeing between the rows of the beet which we had been singling out so laboriously. The Danish horse assigned to me was a gelding called Dagmar. He was huge, but as gentle as a lamb. He and I soon discovered that we spoke a very different language. The English horse will respond happily to the words 'Gee up' which means 'move on' or even to a 'chuck chuck' noise made with the mouth. These two commands seemed to have no effect with Dagmar. He would stand still, turn his head back to look at me and shake his harness impatiently. I had to learn that the English commands to a horse to move off resembled the Danish order to stop. On the other hand the Danish word for the command to 'Go' is very different. It became quite clear that one of us had to learn a new language and Dagmar made it quite obvious that it was not going to be him.

Thorkild, who had been watching from a distance and wondering why he had not yet started work, demonstrated how to make a Danish horse go and, perhaps more importantly, how to stop. Soon Dagmar and I became the best of friends. The language barrier between us quickly evaporated and we shared many hours of happy work together. Just as in past days when I had been able to confide in Haberdashery on the farm in Sussex, Dagmar became my new confidante.

My work experience increased and I was soon able to help raise the Landrace pigs from which the excellent bacon is produced for export. Landrace pigs were bred to produce bacon bearing a minimum of unwanted fat. There is no great mystique to the production of Danish bacon, but success is due to good management and careful breeding. Danish butter is produced from the milk of the practical and productive Danish Red cows. Their milk is skimmed and then fed to the pigs. The cream is then churned into butter at the large cooperative dairies.

Danish farming is methodical and tidy but this led to our working days being long and hard. My body often ached with tiredness. In addition to manual labour, my mind worked hard with the task of learning to master the oral Danish necessary to establish communications with the 'Vikings'. In the evenings, I was taken out to enjoy local events. I was not allowed to leave the farm unless I was wearing my famous red beret. Thus, wherever I went people flocked to shake the hand of Monty the Englander.

Toward the end of my tenure, a shy friendship developed between me and Leila, the daughter of a neighbouring farmer. On one occasion a small travelling circus was visiting Viby and we decided to visit it. Since a group of young men and girls from the local farms had decided to attend as a group, we decided to join their party. Leila's parents gave their permission. In those days, taking a girl out without first seeking the approval of her father was unheard of. Leila was the prettiest of the girls in the group and I sensed some envy emanating from some of the other men.

Soon the excitement generated by the circus dissolved any tension that there might have been. The circus tent was soon packed to capacity. The band, the clowns, and their performing animals paraded around the ring entertaining us. There was a good feeling of community and a great deal of laughter. Suddenly, to my surprise, I was grabbed hold of by two clowns and hustled into the circus ring. A performing horse had been cantering around the ring ridden by an acrobat who had been performing amazing feats of balance, even standing on her head on the saddle of the prancing horse. I had not realised that the Ringmaster had made a challenge to the audience.

"Would someone come forward to ride the performing horse?" The young girl acrobat, resplendent, and very attractive in her sparkling attire, led the prancing pony around the ring. Led by my companions, the crowd began to chant "Monty, Monty, Monty the Englander." Strong hands were propelling me over the barrier into the ring. A body harness was being lowered from the roof of the tent and before I could protest I was being firmly strapped into it. Two clowns jumped onto the back of the horse and clowned their way around the ring to the cheers of the watching crowd. Their demonstration, which included falling off and rolling and jumping around the ring, ended and they gestured to invite me to mount the horse. The honour of England appeared to be at stake, so climbing on top of a wooden stand, willingly hindered by the clowns, I mounted the now docile horse. The clowns slapped it on the backside, and I was off around the ring.

The noise of cheering and laughter was deafening. "Monty, Monty," they chanted. Then their chant changed into screams of delight. I felt myself loosing my grip. I grabbed hold of the horse's mane but I could not keep my balance. I felt myself slipping. I fell and the safety harness swung me to safety. Expecting to be lowered safely to the ground, I was horrified to find myself being hauled up into the very top of the tent, among the trapeze equipment. The band played and the people clapped in rhythm to the music of 'For he's a jolly good fellow' as I dangled high above their heads. Then I was gently lowered to the sawdust of the ring. The Ringmaster shook me vigorously by the hand and I returned to the delighted grins and laughter of my friends. Monty the Englander had served his country, if not bravely, effectively. Leila was very proud of me. Sadly we had been slow and too shy to make friends sooner and in a few days we were to part.

I had been able to save some money because Herr Hansen had generously paid me for my work, although, technically, I had been a participant in a student exchange. My savings enabled me to take a few days holiday. I decided to make my way north to the interesting and beautiful town of Aarhus. Then I made my way south again spending two days visiting the capital city of Copenhagen.

Back at Scosbou, I was sad to leave Viby and my new friends. We all intended to keep in touch. We sincerely meant to try to do so but over the years that followed the contacts eventually eroded. I recall my happy months in Denmark with great affection.

Homeward bound, I travelled by train overland from Denmark, down through Slesvig Holstein, into Germany and on to Cologne. The farmhouses I saw as we travelled still bore the scars of war. Shell holes could be seen in the fields and walls were scored by bullets. Barns had been destroyed and the remains of army trucks and abandoned tanks could be seen as we passed by. Germany was still in the depths of despair after their humiliation by the allied forces.

Cologne Station was guarded by security police. The train was due to stop there for two hours but passengers were not permitted to leave the station. German children, pale and painfully thin, appeared on the platform begging for food and cigarettes. Although I am not a smoker, I had bought some cigarettes because I had been told of their value in Germany. On the platform of Cologne train station a guard approached me for cigarettes. Having received some, he motioned me to follow him. He led me through a door and out into the streets. He guided me across the stricken city of Cologne to the great Cathedral. The destruction had been devastating. I picked my way among the streets surrounding the cathedral accompanied by my silent guide. Like Exeter Cathedral, it had escaped without much damage.

My faithful and silent guide escorted me back to the train just in time to climb aboard before it steamed out of Cologne and continued its journey. We slowly made our way from Germany into France and then to Calais. I can never forget the visit to Cologne. Previously I had only seen the British aspect of the war. I had been in London under fire. I had been spared personal injury or suffering. Now I had glimpsed the immense suffering wrought on the Germans too. I had witnessed the awful destruction wrought on the city of Cologne.

Back in London I reunited with Moo. I still had some Danish krone left which would cover my meagre expenses for a short time. I spent a time of rest and day by day wandered around London's parks and streets, a pastime that I have always enjoyed.

Manor Farm

Moo needed to find a job. The pitiable pension paid to a war widow could never give her adequate financial support. I could not support her as farmhands were the lowest paid of all, and farm students did not even merit pay, but rather were paid pocket money of only a few shillings a week. The remedy for Moo's problem, and the beginning of a new and happier life for her, began when she secured a post as receptionist in the lobby of the headquarters of the National Federation of Women's Institutes in London. 31 Eccleston Street was a hive of activity and Moo was at the centre of it. Her seat at the reception desk was so placed as to see all who entered. At first she was harassed and became extremely tense over the handling of the telephone switchboard, but in time she mastered the complicated 'plug and hole' telephone system and handled it with professional dexterity. Her greeting with a charming and welcoming smile became well known to many who had travelled to London for meetings.

People can here from farms and homes throughout the land. The local pub now took second place in her life and she began to make a great many new friends. I did not realise at the time that the new life that had opened up for her was to affect my own future. Among her new friends was Meryl Withall, at that time Assistant Secretary to the NFWI. She later became the General Secretary. Meryl and Moo became close friends and decided to share a flat together. Having located a suitably pleasant one they settled down together in a comfortable and convenient home situated pleasantly beside Battersea Park.

I felt at home in these surroundings, for, as always, wherever Moo was, home was. She always managed to spoil me by getting my clothes washed, mended and ironed. Now that she was earning a small salary she helped me buy a few new things too.

Moo soon heard of a vacancy on the farm of Sir Digby and Lady Lawson in North Cheriton, Somerset. There was a retired Army officer, Major Neve, in charge and he needed an assistant. I travelled down to Somerset for the interview and was enlisted in Major Neve's army! Unfortunately I was the only soldier and so I was expected to do all the menial work. The Major did not have a huge knowledge about farming either. I soon found the engagement far from satisfactory or happy.

During the few months of this experience I met two people who were to take a leading part in creating the unknown future. One morning, I set out from the farmyard with a white pony called Polly. She was very nervy and had obviously been ill treated. She was not strongly constructed and found being harnessed to a farm cart rather too heavy for her. Like Haberdashery in early days, I managed to make friends with her, and she bravely struggled to accomplish the tasks demanded of her. Being white and working in very muddy fields meant that she looked very dejected and dirty most of the time, although she enjoyed being groomed at the end of the day's work.

One day I noticed a small car draw up over by the field gate. Polly and I were at work. The morning was really filthy. Rain had come down hard all night and it was still coming down with a strong south westerly wind blowing. Our mission was to pull, load, and transport a load of wurzels. Wurzels are a large, round and succulent root, some weighing many pounds, used for cattle feed during the winter months. Both Polly and I were plastered with mud such as only a Somerset field can supply. Polly was so caked in it that she could have been mistaken for a brown horse!

A tall figure, in a black mackintosh raincoat, was stumbling and staggering across the flooded ground towards me. As he drew close, I saw to my surprise that it was the local Vicar. He came up to me and introduced himself. "My name's Langley," he said. "I heard that there was a new man at Manor Farm and I just thought I'd come across and welcome you to the village." He held out his hand in friendship. My hands were wet, very cold, and extremely dirty. As he noticed my hesitation to respond to his proffered hand he laughed and said, "Michael, shake hands with me. A little good honest dirt never hurt anybody." We shook hands, and I realised that here was an honest friend. "How about coming to lunch on Sunday, after church?" he suggested. I was due in London for a day off, and explained that usually lunch was not a good time for me because I would have to wash and change in the middle of a working day. Canon Tom Langley was not one to be put off. "How about breakfast, then?" he insisted. "Come in your working clothes before you start work."

"I start at five in the morning," I answered. There was a moment's silence.

"What time do you have breakfast then?" he countered.

"It's at eight o'clock, and on Sundays I'll have finished until milking time in the afternoon," I confided.

"That's *my* busy day," he replied. "Why not come to breakfast at eight on Saturday and let the Major clean up after milking." This was said with a mischievous grin. How could I refuse? A friendship with Tom Langley and his dear and charming wife, Monica, was to be of the greatest significance for my future.

Breakfast led to an invitation to learn to be a bell ringer. I was not too keen to be involved in the life of the local church. The bell ringers however were a happy group of men from the village and surrounding farms. The art of bell ringing proved to be beyond my ability. I was far too nervous to properly handle the vigorous activity of pulling the rope and the tassel, called a Sally. The Sally was made of wool, and the weight of the bell high in the rafters meant that the ringer had to exercise considerable skill and timing in order to keep the bell from getting out of control. The rope could become dangerous. It is claimed that people have been killed by the whipping and lashing of a bell rope. I failed to attend future bell practices.

Katherine Daniel, a lady who farmed nearby Manor Farm and a leading light in the local Women's Institute, had also been alerted to my presence in the village. Another breakfast, the first of many, led to a special friendship with her. This was also to have tremendous importance in the future. My new friends both felt that Manor Farm was not the right place for me and that it would not help my ongoing climb up the farming ladder. Moo had mentioned my plight to friends in the W.I. and a new contact was made with a well known farming family in Somerset.

The Hebditch family had farmed at Newcross Farm, South Petherton for several generations. Mr. Hebditch, the senior, had recently retired and his son, John, needed an experienced Assistant to help with the herd of Ayrshire milking cows. A successful interview resulted from a happy visit at Newcross Farm. With the enthusiastic encouragement and support from both Tom and Monica Langley, as well as from Katharine Daniel, I faced Major Neve and told him that I was leaving Manor Farm. My arrival at Newcross Farm heralded the start of a new and happier phase of my life.

Newcross Farm

My initial visit to the farm for the interview had left me in no doubt as to the future. John and Marjorie Hebditch had three young daughters, Sally, Kathleen and Mary. We all seemed to get on well and I was excited about the invitation to join them. I was to live as part of the family and help John manage the dairy herd of Ayrshire cows as well as share in other general farm work as needed.

The Hebditch family quickly made me feel at home and I was treated as one of their charming family. While the days were long and the work was hard, life with the Hebditch family was different. They cared about me as had Tom and Monica Langley and Katherine Daniel.

On Sundays, the seven day chore of milking the cows and caring for their needs was the only job to be done. The family would soon be adorned in their Sunday best and make their way to the historic Congregation Chapel at Middle Labour. While I was invited to join them I found myself longing to, but for some reason I held back from doing so. I have often wondered why I resisted their invitation to join them in Sunday worship. One reason was my hesitation to intrude into what was so clearly a very important family tradition each week. They were so completely sincere in their hope that I would join them, but I stayed at home.

Whilst no one was there, I would go into their comfortable sitting room in which John had always lit the fire, ready for their return from chapel. Making my way to the piano, I would play all my favourite melodies. I even picked out tunes from the hymnal on the piano stand. After a while I would turn to the Sunday newspaper. When the family returned, I would sometimes be found fast asleep by the cosy fire.

The principal reason for my decision to decline their invitation was undoubtedly a form of escapism, tinged with the feeling that I was a member of a different church. I was a member of the Church of England. But my membership was nominal. Despite my recent friendship with Tom Langley and the fact that I ending up attending his church on a few occasions, I had little desire to take part in what I considered an out of date and very monotonous activity. I began to think very deeply concerning what I called to myself 'the deeper side of life'.

Traditional Sunday lunch was the main meal of the week, and there was much fun and laughter around the table as we shared the events on the farm and in the district. During the meal plans were made for the week to come.

I joined the Young Farmer's Club and that widened my horizons. I belonged to a team that won the Public Speaking Competition. I was also asked to write some short articles about farming. They were published in the Girl Guide magazine and one was published in the Girl Guide Annual.

John and Marjorie encouraged me to persevere with new interests. Having some form of independent transport became necessary; so with John's help, I bought a motor bike. I was now receiving fare and full payment for my services as John's assistant, in charge of the dairy herd.

One Sunday morning, I made my way to a tiny chapel I had noticed. The chapel was attached to an ancient Abbey. A Vicar came there once a week to celebrate the Holy Communion Service. Only a few people were present and I felt uneasy as I tried to recall my confirmation training by Dean Youard at St. Mary's Church in Battle, Sussex all those years before. I took my place in the pew, which to my embarrassment creaked loudly every time I shifted my weight or changed my position from sitting, to kneeling, to standing.

When the time came for me to receive the little sacramental piece of bread and sip the wine, I was so nervous I felt as if I might feint. The perspiration was dripping from my forehead. The service was being intoned in the tradition that was common in the church in those days, but the words began to move me tremendously. '*And to all thy people give thy heavenly grace*'. The prayer pointed me towards my first understanding that there appeared to be a difference between people who followed in the footsteps of the Lord God. Are there two ways through life? I wondered. Are there two kinds of people? What, I wondered, really is heavenly grace?

This was only the beginning. I was becoming more aware of a need for deeper comprehension of life. Men and women like Tom and Monica Langley, Katherine Daniel and the Hebditch family were changing my attitude. Why did they care about me?

The quiet and humble presentation of the Book of Common Prayer's service, The Order of the Lord's Supper or Holy Communion, which culminated in the gift of a tiny wafer of bread and a sip of wine, brought me an unreasonable sense of well being. Despite my introduction to the beliefs of the Christian faith at school, I had little understanding why they should do so.

A different, but newly realised, spirit of adventure prompted me to join a local unit of the Territorial Army. The officers and men of 663 Super Heavy Regiment, Royal Artillery, were a very different experience for me. Gunner Bishop would make his way once a week to Drill Night. I was assigned for training for service in the Forward Observation Post.

I soon realised that I'd been chosen for a somewhat dangerous role. The big gun had a range of about twenty miles but a forward position was necessary in order to locate targets and then give accurate directions to the gunner's miles behind us. I hoped that the training would never be called upon for action in real conflict, but the post war tension between the Western Powers and the Soviet Union made it very possible that we might one day be enlisted for full time service. I so enjoyed the fellowship and, especially, the annual two week training camp at Larkhill on Salisbury Plain that I seriously considered making application to join the Regular Army. But my Army service, and for a time my farming too, were to end abruptly.

One June evening, at tea time, a telephone call came through from the regiment that I was needed. The cricket team had an engagement against the Yeovil Bus Company and was a man short. Could I possibly fill the gap? We had been very hard at work making hay while the sun shone all day but a shower of rain had curtailed work for the day and I was free to respond in the affirmative. I had not played any cricket for a long time, but my early training in the garden in Sussex and at school had not been forgotten. During the match, I had become something of a hero. I had rescued our team from disaster by hitting thirty-two runs. One of my hits of the ball was hard and I sent the ball racing towards the boundary for four runs. Yet as I struck the ball, I felt a searing pain in my knee. I fell to the ground with intense pain. I knew that I had sustained a serious injury. I was carried off the pitch on a stretcher and soon found myself in Yeovil Hospital.

That injury was to change my life. The knee joint was severely damaged, the medial tendon almost severed, and the cartilage needed removal. My farming days were over for a while. When it became apparent that it would take a long time to recover from the injury, it was decided that I should say farewell to the Hebditchs and Newcross Farm, at least for the time being. I moved to London to live with my mother and Meryl in their flat. I then went under the care of the orthopaedic department at St. Georges Hospital, Hyde Park Corner, London.

Knee surgery followed and a long period was spent with my right leg strapped to a board. At first I struggled about on crutches and later I managed with a walking stick. The surgeon, a Mr. Rowlands, who was also in the Territorial Army serving as Medical Registrar, told me that he would have to fix my leg so that it would be permanently stiff. He informed me that I should make up my mind that I could no longer undertake farm work. He also arranged for me to be retired from the Territorial Army as unfit for further service and to receive a lump sum payment of £50 as compensation since the injury had occurred whilst engaged in TA activities!

My world had been torn apart. I had no thoughts as to what I should do in the future. The brief period of security and happiness with the Hebditch family had ended. It seemed unlikely that I would be able to continue my now happy and successful climb up the farming ladder. I had to face the possibility seeking a new career in which no heavy manual work would be required.

Battersea Carousel

The days since the end of the war had been depressing and grey. Queues for bread had been common place and, for a time, rationing had returned. It seemed as if old England would never shrug off the apathy which had fallen so heavily upon her since the victory celebrations in 1945. The Labour Government of Mr. Harold Wilson organised the Festival of Britain to counter this mood. They set up the centre piece for this enterprising promotion within sight of Moo's flat in Battersea Park, on the bank of the Thames River. The Festival was intended to lift the spirit and the economy of the nation.

Albert Bridge, that strangely attractive suspension bridge which links affluent Chelsea to a then very dreary and run down Battersea, was adorned with coloured lights and provided an entry point for many visitors. As part of the festival a Fun Fair had been established in Battersea Park, in the shadow of the massive Battersea Power Station. The noise of the organ emanating from the large carousel created the beginnings of a festive spirit for post war-weary Londoners, and their visitors.

My knee had taken time to heal and was never to regain full and trouble free mobility again. I wandered the streets of London, day after day, returning every evening with a sore and swollen knee. Moo tried her best to cheer me up. My farming career was apparently at a close as I had failed to find a way forward in the small minded management offices of the farming co-operative business. I was bereft of ideas, bored, and probably very irritable. I was not a happy person. This was a time when I stood in need of a friend of my own age. For a few weeks a young Welsh nurse, named Pam, who I had met in the orthopaedic department at St. Georges Hospital provided a caring and sympathetic ear to my troubles. She was small and solid, rather like a Welsh pony which was in contrast to Valerie, who was athletic, tall and in comparison to Pam, a thoroughbred!

One afternoon, I invited Pam to come to tea. She endeared herself to Moo when, noticing that my shoe lace was loose, her nursing training caused her to kneel to tie it for me. We went to see one or two movies together and to the west end London theatres to see some of the shows of the period. Our friendship remained platonic. I valued this relationship very much and, but for a renewed contact with Valerie, it might have blossomed into something more romantic.

Once again, the family tradition of patronizing the local pub was to come to my aid. Pubs have traditionally been centres for social caring and never seemed to let me down. The chatter of the regular customers and the feeling of belonging, which is a feature associated with the best English pubs, would accumulate to create an experience which it is difficult to describe.

Into the smoky and beery atmosphere of the Price Albert pub, near Albert Bridge, came each evening an elderly man with his Jack Russell terrier. The little dog would perform tricks in return for a free pint of beer for her master. One evening there, we met an aristocratic gentleman. He was drawn into the conversation when he heard us discussing the activities in Battersea Park. He told us that he was the Personnel Manager for the Fun Fair and that there were quite a number of jobs to be had for anyone who might be interested. I listened as he explained that the travelling show men, who had been invited to bring their fair ground equipment to Battersea, were under an agreement to share fifty percent of their takings with the Festival management.

The monies that they were handing over to the management appeared to be very little when compared with the numbers of the public being admitted to the Fun Fair each day. He was looking for local people who would be interested in temporary employment. Their job would be to check the numbers of those taking rides on the various swings and roundabouts. I felt Moo nudging my arm and knew that she was trying to encourage me to overcome my shyness. Timidly, I told him that I was looking for a job. I was invited to go and see him in his office in the morning.

By ten o'clock next day, I was an employee of the Festival of Britain. I was assigned to the carousel owned by Mr. Harry Gray, one of the showmen. The hobby horses, spinning around to the rhythmic music of the barrel-organ were a popular ride with all ages. My job was to sit on a stationary platform in the centre of all this spinning humanity and count the number of riders on each session. Each ride took approximately three minutes. There would be up to eighty riders each time. Mr. Grey would have to pay half total takings to the Festival Committee. He would watch my estimate of riders and scowl at me when he thought I had miscounted. Practice makes perfect and I was soon a reliable ride checker.

I was earning £15 a week, which was considerably more than I would have been earning in farming. I was allowed two breaks of forty five minutes during the day, a marvellous relief from the spinning horses and riders. During those breaks I would wander around Battersea Park. The lake and the gardens had been carefully recreated to provide a pleasant area in which to relax.

One stall caught my attention. A catchy song was emanating from it, advertising a cartoon character of the day, Muffin the Mule. The music ended, and a voice which I though I recognised called, "Won't you buy a muffin, Sir? Come and see." A wooden muffin was being demonstrated. Having a magnetic nose, its head followed the metallic carrot which was being offered to it by its tall and charming demonstrator. "Come on, sir! Buy a muffin to take home to your sweetheart!"

Curious to find out whom it was attracting my attention so determinedly I pushed through the crowds to see. To my astonishment it was Valerie. Never lacking in initiative, she too had travelled to London to stay with a friend in some flats near Battersea Park and now was established in the sales department of Muffin! I have since suspected that Moo, seeing that I was in the process of striking up a new friendship with the nurse, had tipped off Valerie that perhaps she should come and renew her claims on me. If so, her actions were a blessing. Our friendship of so many years matured day by day and we had a great deal of fun together; meeting for our breaks from work and relaxing and sharing our evenings.

One morning, Mr. Grey came aboard the carousel and into my small cubicle in the centre of the ride. To my surprise, he presented me with a bottle of champagne as a token of his thanks, he said, for my work. He inferred that there would be a great many gifts to come if I were to fail to count the riders so accurately. He would even give me a generous bonus at the end of each week. This was a clear attempt to bribe me into cheating my employers. I declined his gift and spurned his offer as politely as I could. I imagined that he thought very little of me after that, but I was wrong.

I had been yearning to return to my life in the countryside and an opening managing a farm for a distant relative of Valerie's family had arisen. The time had come for a decision and I decided that I would like to see if my much improved knee would stand up to a less rigorous life back on the farm. Having tendered my resignation, I went to see Mr. Grey to thank him for having put up with me as the official checker on his ride. He asked me what I was going to do next. When I told him that I was going back to farming, he became thoughtful.

"Young man," he said, "how about working for me, full time. I could do with a chap like you. I'd pay you well and provide you with your own van. I like your honesty and I need someone to join my travelling fair. You would be responsible for collecting all the monies taken on the rides, checking that the boys turn it all in, counting, and banking it. You'll travel the land, and the continent and lead a free and interesting life."

I was intrigued with the idea of becoming a traveller, with my own home on wheels. I had seen the showmen's quarters. They were like palaces on wheels. Perhaps it would be a fascinating life. I thanked him and said I'd like to think it over. My relationship with Valerie had progressed to the point where we considered whether we should get married quickly, and take to the road with Harry Gray and his associates. This was an exciting prospect, but as the days went by it became less and less appealing to us. Mr. Grey would have to look around for another honest man.

Lulworth Cove

My work at Festival Gardens had given me my first taste of a better paid job, but it was only temporary. I had still not been able to accumulate any savings and I had to find work as soon as possible. As my search for a job ended in deadlock time and time again, I often thought about Harry Gray's offer of a new beginning and life on the open road with his travelling Fun Fair.

I retraced my footsteps and revisited the Hebditch family. It was wonderful to visit Newcross Farm again and spend some time with this dear farming family. John, who was always a good listener as well as a voluble talker, asked if I had thought of working on one of the cooperative trading societies that served the farming community. John enthusiastically stated that he had good contacts with them. He suggested that we go to see the manager of the local Branch Office where he purchased most of his feed seeds and fertilisers that were used on the farm.

I climbed aboard John's Land Rover which felt just like the old days. We made our way to Crewkerne through the leafy lanes of Somerset that I had come to love so much. I realised more than ever how much I missed life on the farm.

All farmers drive erratically and our journey was no exception! Punctuated with stops and sudden swerves to avoid oncoming traffic, I watched John crane his neck over the hedgerows to see what was going on in the fields of his neighbours or just to check out his own flock of sheep. Fortunately we arrived safely at the office of the Farmer's Cooperative Society in the small town of Crewkerne.

"There are no openings at our local branch here in Crewkerne", John's friend, the Manager, said. He added "But I do know there's a vacancy in Dorchester." His hand reached out for the telephone. After a brief word of introduction and a short chat he put the phone down. "Mr. Weller, the Managing Director of Dorset Farmers, would like you to go and see him, Michael. Could you get up to see him tomorrow?" I nodded enthusiastically.

The following morning I began to make my way to Dorchester. I looked forward to seeing the town made famous by the author and poet Thomas Hardy. Could this be the beginning of a new adventure, I wondered. I enjoyed my ride down on my Matchless 500 motorcycle. The road between Somerset and

Dorchester takes you through some of the prettiest scenery in western England. The sight of the newly sown wheat or a beautiful herd of dairy cows increased my longing to return to some connection with farming. The beauty around me caused me to sing and shout for joy as I rode along.

Mr. Weller was a solid character. He listened to my story, outlined the job that he had to offer and warmly invited me to join his company. I would be a trainee salesman. My pay would be about the same amount as I had received at the Festival Gardens. I would start work in the Head Office in Dorchester in order to 'learn the ropes'. Later, when I had learned about the business I would become a salesman. I would have my own Dorset Farmers van in which I would go from farm to farm taking orders for farm seeds, foodstuffs, chemicals and fertilisers. The job sounded as if it were an excellent opportunity and I was thrilled when Mr. Weller put out his hand and said, "so, when can you start, Michael?" We agreed that I could take up my new job as soon as possible.

I needed somewhere to live so I reserved a room in a hotel, the Casterbridge, which catered for commercial travellers and young men on business in the town. I promptly reported to work full of hope and intending to become the best salesman ever. I knew the farming business well. I believed that a new career was beginning.

The office was set out in three departments. The most 'important' area, almost a godlike sanctuary, was Mr. Weller's, the Managing Director. I only entered it twice during the twelve months of my stay—on my first day and my last! The Manager's office was just a little more accessible than Mr. Weller's. Here Mr. Trowell sat at a tall Dickensian clerk's desk. A glass partition separated him from the general office. The general office contained three desks. At one, sat Ray Moore, the Head Clerk; next to him a secretary, Sue, a pretty girl who always managed to look fresh and lovely as she sat in the limelight beneath the watchful eye of Mr. Trowell; and desk three was for me.

Ray's job was to read every communication that came into the office. Farmers' orders, invoices, communications from all the branch offices, and the head office of the Cooperative Wholesale Society came under his scrutiny. My desk was bare. No telephone, no typewriter, nothing.

"Punctuality is important. You will be expected to be at your desk by nine. Lunch hour is from one to two, and the office closes at five." Instructions from Mr. Trowell were brief and to the point. No smile, no welcome, just a stern call to work and efficiency!

Ray was much friendlier. I knew that I would like him as we shook hands. Sue gave me a shy smile. I thought I detected a touch of amusement and compassion in her eyes as she grinned and said "Hello".

The phone in Mr. Trowell's office rang incessantly. Ray's phone would buzz when they needed to chat busily from their ivory towers of management. Pieces of paper would be passed through a sliding glass window to Ray, who would pass them to Sue, who then set to work with her typewriter. I noticed that she sat with a very straight back and thought that she had obviously trained in an excellent school for secretaries. Sue passed the invoices onto my empty desk. Invoice after invoice began to flow, and accumulate in front of me. Ray leant over my shoulder. "How's your maths, Mike?" he inquired with a mischievous grin. "Because your job is to check out all these figures very carefully and if you find any mistakes just pass the invoice back to me for correction."

I was shattered. If I had any talents, accuracy in adding, subtracting, multiplying and dividing were not amongst them. In the late 1940s there were no calculators in the office. They hadn't been invented. I began the task very nervously. My slow, methodical ploughman's brain began to respond to the challenge. As the pile of paper grew larger, my spirit sank into a deep depression. How long would I have to be in the office in order to 'learn the ropes', I wondered!

A month or two went by before I summoned up the courage to question Ray. "When will I get out of the office", I pleaded. He explained that I had to wait for an opening, and counselled patience. There were no sales territories vacant.

In the meantime, Sue, having a quick and sharp mind, came to my rescue. Getting through her own work at record speed she began to snatch invoices off my desk and pass them, checked, back into Ray's in-tray. My burden was greatly eased and my anxiety and weariness relieved, although I found each day that passed to be extremely boring.

Sue and I often decided to take our lunch hour together. We would relax in each other's company and enjoy passing the time away in idle chatter. Sue was not on my mind though. A catchy tune about Muffin the Mule, evoking memories of my recent time with Valerie in Festival Gardens, was constantly on my mind. I imagined that I could hear Valerie's voice calling out to me, "Won't you buy a muffin!" Fortunately, we had been keeping in touch by exchanging letters and sharing our stories.

We agreed that I should visit Valerie. The time arrived for Velossopop, the name we have given my motor bike, to take me down to visit her. I was welcomed at her home as a member of a family. These trips became more frequent. My journeys across the Dorset Downs to their new home, Exton Mill, near Topsham, strengthened the bond between us and our relationship grew deeper. At work, day followed day, and week followed week.

Still I persevered with my boring work of checking invoices. As my mind sharpened I became quick to detect errors in the cascade of invoices which showered onto my desk. Sometimes I was rewarded with an encouraging smile from the observant Mr. Trowell, who looked down on me as if I was a lower kind of being from his exalted seat on the other side of the glass partition.

There was little social life in Dorchester to brighten evenings. The other residents at the hotel appeared to live in a world of their own. They all smoked heavily and spent their evenings checking long columns of order sheets, or reading seamy novels. I would go to bed early and listen to my portable radio. The proprietor's wife would come to my door and bellow "Keep the sound of that radio down please!" I would bury it under my bedclothes.

The stale smell of cigarette smoke infiltrated under the door. My bedclothes and the air in my room absorbed the stale aroma of other peoples smoke. While the odour permeated the whole hotel, my complaints about it went unheard.

Velossopop helped to brighten my weekends. I explored Dorset ranging from Dorchester, past Maiden Castle, the ancient British encampment on the Dorset Downs, and over to Weymouth. I could imagine how interesting having my own sales territory and visiting the farms would be.

Ray was concerned about my arid and unpleasant way of life at the Casterbridge Hotel. Mr. and Mrs. Vic Pomeroy, his neighbours, had offered to take me in as their lodger. Their home was in one of the 1930's type housing estates of Dorchester. Vic Pomeroy was a big man in every sense. He looked like a storybook characterization of one in his occupation—a butcher. He had rosy cheeks which highlighted a cheerful smile. The rotund framework of his body advertised the excellence of the produce from the shop that he managed. Mrs. Pomeroy was a cheerful person. Although I could call Vic by his first name, Mrs. Pomeroy always remained Mrs. Pomeroy. To this day I have no idea what her first name was. The hearty breakfasts, delicious packed lunches, and magnificent high teas, restored my ribbed skeleton, spindly legs, and pale complexion. And all these services came at half the cost of the room at the hotel!

What a joy it was to have my own front door key. Sharing the open fire in the small living room and having good friends to share the evening with was wonderful. Together, we enjoyed the ritual of hearing the weather forecast and the BBC's six o'clock news.

Vic had been a Chief Petty Officer in the Royal Navy and his morning call to start my day still rings in my ears as it had once done for his sleepy sailors. "Wakey, wakey, the sun's up, and ready to burn your eyeballs out!"

One day I heard from somewhere a Miss Lang was looking for a young man who would be willing to give her some part-time help in her beautiful garden. I knew little about gardening but the prospect of doing some manual work, which I had missed since the accident to my knee, appealed to me greatly. Miss Lang was a kind elderly lady. I was told that she was the sister of the Archbishop of Canterbury, Cosmo Lang. She lived in Hardy's Cottage in Higher Bockhampton, just outside Dorchester. The cottage was the home of Thomas Hardy and is now part of the National Trust. She made me very welcome and in exchange for a little pocket money, I enjoyed many a fine evening digging and weeding the flower beds in the tranquil setting of the cottage's garden.

One Saturday, Valerie came to Dorchester for the day by bus. We decided to go out into the Dorsetshire countryside on my motor cycle. Valerie enjoyed the thrill and speed experienced on the pillion seat of Velossopop. From that time on Vic Pomeroy insisted on referring to that seat as the 'flapper bracket'.

Our friendship turned into romance; the seeds of friendship and trust sown years before at The Traveller's Rest had taken root and grown. On that sunny Saturday morning we set out to explore the Dorset coast. We made for a beautiful spot known to Valerie—Lulworth Cove. To this day, Lulworth Cove is place full of memories and a site to which we have often returned.

We climbed the cliffs to a spot high above the cove. We were both strangely silent and I was, as ever, feeling shy. I had great many things on my mind. I realised, deep down, that my loneliness was over and that I was in love. In my earlier year girls had not found an enduring place and since I attended an all boy Preparatory school, I was poorly prepared for all the emotions that I was experiencing. Whatever I had learned about romance must have come from Hollywood movies! Here was someone that I could trust; one whose tall, athletic looks, mischievous sense of humour, basic commonsense, and deep compassion blended perfectly. When I was with Valerie I felt utterly relaxed and in harmony.

We sat holding hands, in awe at the emotions within us. The beauty around us was magnificent. Valerie was unusually silent. The shadows lengthened and I could no longer suppress the yearning within me. My heart thumped as if trying to break out of my rib cage, frustrated with the hesitancy of the young man whose body it powered. Then, I took that great leap of faith that must begin the pathway towards marriage. "I love you. Will you marry me?" I gasped.

We reached out for each other and held one another. The quiet answer came "Yes". And then, after a moment, she murmured "I thought you were never going to ask me."

We hugged our way back to Dorchester and discussed how to break our exciting news to our parents and friends. We were in a state of wonder and exhilaration. Life was great. This was a time of joy and liberation for both of us. But we were both without any savings and we knew that the path towards our wedding day would be much steeper than the climb up the cliffs to this, our piece of hallowed ground high up overlooking Lulworth Cove.

Perrotts Brook

Moo's position, as receptionist at the front desk of the National Federation of Women's Institutes in Ebury Street, near Victoria Station in London, together with her local pub in Battersea, continued to form the hub of her personal intelligence service. Here she met and made friends with country people from all over England. She kept closely in touch with Mrs. W. H. Hebditch, the matriarch of the farming family based at Newcross Farm in East Lambrook, Somerset. Through this labyrinth of contacts, information concerning potential jobs for her younger son was received.

In the spring of 1952 an exciting possibility emerged from this network. A well known countryman and industrialist, Sir John Langman, was looking for a young man to manage his two hundred and forty acre farm at Perrotts Brook, near Cirencester, in Gloucestershire. He had heard my name mentioned. The contacts within the Somerset, or 'Hebditch', area concerned for my future had been at work. Sir John would like to meet me. 'Me' now included Valerie too! We were engaged and deeply in love with no where to go! Sir John and Lady Pamela invited us down to stay at their Cotswold home.

Perrotts Brook house was situated on a bank overlooking the River Churn at North Cerney. The farm cottages and buildings lay a short distance down a narrow and leafy lane from the house. Below the farm buildings were green and lush water meadows. Through them the little River Churn meandered peacefully on its journey through the Cotswold Hills. On its way, the river would become more and more important, eventually flowing into the River Thames, which rises at Thames Head in the hills above the town of Cheltenham.

The farm was comprised of a Mill House, a barn and a few farm cottages. The Mill House sat beside a leat, down which rushed an ever present volume of fast flowing water. Many years before the leat had driven a water wheel which, in turn, had powered a corn mill. The Mill House was set aside for the Farm Manager. Nearby were two farm cottages for farm staff to live in. The tractor driver and his family, and the cowman, had cottages too.

The farm land lay along the river, and rose from there, up sloping ground to the hill top. The Roman road, the Fosse Way, formed part of the farm's boundary. The farm land was divided into a harmony of fields of various sizes, divided by those ancient, picturesque, and practical dry stone walls so familiar in Cotswold country. If well built by skilled wallers, these walls had withstood perhaps a hundred years of use. Across the Fosse Way a plateau of larger land farmed by Mr. Nigel Anstee, the next door neighbour, stretched away into the distance.

Home Farm, part of the Bathurst Estate to which this area belonged, was nearby nestled beside the Churn, and formed part of the charming village of North Cerney. Across the road from the Bathurst Arms pub, the village inn and the ancient parish church of North Cerney completed the trilogy that created the wholeness of old England's country life—farm, pub and church—farmer, landlord and vicar. All that had to be added to further augment this team were the village policeman, the doctor and the midwife. All the needs of the small population were adequately met without the huge cost of social services or expensive medical facilities.

Valerie and I were invited to stay with the Langmans at Perrotts Brook. We found it hard to believe that this opportunity was being presented to us. Sir John, and Lady Pamela, both very typical of the Gloucestershire country and fox hunting community, made us feel very much at ease. After a welcome cup of tea, Sir John took us for a walking tour of the farm and buildings. The herd of pedigree Jersey cows were on their way in for milking in the modern milking parlour, and it was obvious that they were the main interest to their proud owners. Sir John was greeting and patting the individual and aristocratic looking cows of the herd by personal name. He explained that the farm belonged to the estate owned by Lord Bathurst. Although Sir John owned farms in Cadbury, down in Somerset, he had been able to rent Perrotts Brook from Lord Bathurst. This location was convenient for him because he was a Director of Newman Hender, an industrial manufacturer based at Nailsworth, a few miles away. Sir John would commute from Perrots Brook to work there each morning.

Sir John been raised on the family farms in Cadbury. As an adult he found that he needed to have a farm nearby on which to relax as there was nothing he liked more than to be involved in the daily business of farm life. He was often absent from work and farm life though, as he made extensive travels abroad. Consequently there was a job opening for a young man who wanted to gain a foothold and make a career in farm management. Sir John became interested in me when he had heard that although I was not college trained and did not have a degree in agriculture, I had a great deal of practical experience on some very well known and forward looking farms. He had been making inquiries and assured me, kindly, that the references that he had been given were very excellent.

Our long and exhausting farm walk took place on a lovely early summer's day. I wondered if my injured knee would stand up to the rigors of hill walking up and down the Cotswolds. But it did and I was able to relax. After showering and changing in the luxurious guest room, Valerie and I joined the Langmans for dinner.

After dinner, Sir John offered me the job. The salary offered was disappointingly low, at £7–10 shillings a week. The compensation sounded better when it was explained that it included a rent free house, the Mill House, free milk, wood from the farm, coal and electricity. Sir John suggested that if I decided to take up his offer an initial trial period of three months would determine both whether he was confident in my farming ability and, for my part, that I was comfortable and happy in my relationship with him.

"So now," he concluded kindly, "you and Valerie can go into the garden, and enjoy the evening sitting on our sun lounger. Then let me know your decision in the morning. If you would like to come to us, then after the period of three months, all being well, you and Valerie could get married and look forward to the years ahead with us.

My head was spinning with excitement, but could I ever fulfil Sir John's expectations? He explained that he wanted me to farm as if it was my own farm, but in partnership with him. He loved the farm, but would not interfere, except with suggestions to experiment with new ideas. As an afterthought he added, "And by the way, we need to make a loss." Since food production had a high priority at that time, the government provided substantial tax benefits to those farming industrialists who were high tax payers, but were investing in Britain's farms.

Valerie and I held hands, swung gently on the garden seat. We talked into the small hours of the night. In the morning during breakfast, at the age of 25, I became the new farm manager at Perrotts Brook Farm.

Wedding Bells

The farm manager's cottage, Mill House, needed both repairs and regeneration. So on taking up my duties Sir John had reserved a room for me at the Bear Inn. Being on the main Cheltenham to Cirencester road and close to the farm, the pub location was ideal. After all, I had been dependent on pubs throughout my life!

The landlord and his wife were very welcoming. My little bedroom, complete with a china washbasin and water jug was warm and cosy. There was even a chamber pot under the bed. This was just the place to return to after a hard days work on the farm. If I needed company there was always the chatter and ongoing life of the pub to enjoy. But I was soon to discover that I would have little time to spend in the bar challenged to a game of darts or dominoes with my new friends. Bed and breakfast would be all the time I could spend in what I hoped would be only temporary quarters.

Back on the farm I was anxious to meet the farm workers who would have to accept this young manager into their midst. Ron, the cowman, cared for and milked the precious Churnside herd of pedigree Jersey cows. He soon became known to me as a pleasant and capable man. The cows and their welfare were his territory and I could see that he was ready to defend his 'cow kingdom'. He wielded a great deal of power. My first job would be to gain his confidence.

I set out to study the individual members of the herd, getting to recognise them individually. I tried to link them with their progeny. The best heifer calves were selected as suitable for future breeding stock. They were the daughters of Bargower, the bull, and his harem. Bargower was the pride and prize of Sir John's heart. He had cost a great deal of money and I knew that he was more important to Sir John than all the tea in China!

The amount of milk drawn from each cow each time she was milked was weighed and recorded. I gathered the record books and smuggled them back to the pub each evening to study and memorise the details of each individual animal. During the day I continued to work hard to recognise each animal and call them by name. Soon I could greet each member of the bovine family by name and link them with their daughters. The heifer calves lived in the lap of luxury in their well strawed and cosy calf pens.

Stan, the tractor driver and general worker, also knew his job. The standard of his work was as good as I had seen anywhere at the other farms I had experience on my farming ladder. I knew that it would be hard to win his respect as I would not be able to match his skill. I could tell that I had a challenging future ahead of me if I was to gain Sir John's confidence and be invited to take up residence in the Mill House, with the possibility of a new farm manager's wife in residence also.

Back at the Bear Inn I encountered what I can only believe was a ghost. One night I became very frightened. I don't know whether I was awake or dreaming. I felt as if someone had climbed onto my bed and then onto my back. Whatever it was weighed a lot and felt like a small person. I was terrified and though I was a very strong and tough young man I could not free myself. I struggled to throw whoever, or whatever, it was off me, but to no avail. I don't know how long I must have lain there unable to move. Suddenly there was a loud bump on the floor and the weight was lifted. I climbed out of bed expecting perhaps that some animal had been in the room but it was empty. I lay awake for the rest of the night. In the morning I decided to keep my experience to myself. It was not until many years later when I had left the area that I told a friend, who knew the Bear Inn well, about my experience. I learned that he had heard that a man had committed suicide in that room. I am glad that no one told me so while I was still resident in the pub.

The days, weeks and months at the farm sped by. I was so involved in my task of managing the farm through the spring of the year and the summer, with little free time to spare, that I had little time to visit Valerie in Devonshire. The day to day planning needed to farm an intensive dairy farm can be very complicated and frustrating. A farmer's factory has no roof. The preparation of the arable land and the sowing of the seeds, whether corn, grass, or kale, that were all an essential part of the economy for a dairy business, required, all the skill and patience that I'd acquired so far in my quest to become a good farmer.

The three months which Sir John and I agreed were a trial period for both of us soon passed. I enjoyed the dinner and breakfast meetings with the boss each week, and walked the farm with him each weekend, but not a word passed between us about my future. As we developed our plans for the autumn and the harvest one morning at our weekly breakfast, I took the courage to broach the subject that had become topmost in my and Valerie's minds.

"I've just realised that my three month trial period as your manager expired some weeks ago Sir," I began. Sir John looked up from his plateful of bacon and eggs.

"Oh, Michael," he said, "of course, I'm so sorry. I quite forgot. Poor Valerie." After a short time he added "You'd better get married as soon as possible." The relief was tremendous and the excitement almost overwhelming. "Use my telephone now and tell Valerie you can get married as soon as you like," he concluded.

We decided to marry in the delightful church of Saint Swithin, in the village of Woodbury in Devon on October 4, 1952. The Vicar, the Reverend Alec Osmond, prepared us for marriage. As part of his instruction he used a small china cockerel and hen to represent the couple at the altar and to instruct us in the meaning of the Christian marriage. I felt deeply moved by the love and wisdom shown by this bachelor priest. Little was I to know that one day I, too, would prepare couples for marriage. I even ended up following Alec Osmond's example by using china ornaments to represent the bride and groom!

When the day arrived, the setting could not have been any more charming for a farmer's wedding. Saint Swithin's was already decorated for the harvest festival services to be held the following day. My mother, Moo, was there looking rather sombre in her only church outfit, which had seen her through more funerals than weddings. Edward, my best man, gave the support expected from an elder brother. Valerie, escorted by her proud father and supported by her two best friends, Finetta Campbell and Rosemary Safford, arrived at the church twenty minutes late. She looked gorgeous in her wedding gown. She later told me that she and her father had stopped beside a field gate and watched a pair of rabbits playing. I wondered if it had been some kind of last minute counsel and instruction concerning the facts of life.

Like so many bridegrooms, I have difficulty in remembering much detail about the marriage service. I would have preferred to be quickly back at Perrotts Brook, getting on with the farm work without, what I considered to be, all the fuss. The words of the marriage service, however, and the loving and reverent way in which we were joined together served to overcome any unchristian cynicism that might have threatened to spoil the day for me. Valerie and I trembled together as we absorbed the fact that we were husband and wife.

The sun shone and the reception, held in the local pub, the George and Dragon, was a happy occasion. I overheard Sir John and Lady Langman telling Moo that they were glad that I eventually had the courage to inquire whether my work was considered satisfactory and my appointment confirmed. Jack and

Audrey, Valerie's parents provided a generous wedding feast for us. Champagne was flowing freely, but for some reason the landlord of the George and Dragon neglected to make sure that the bride and groom received the bubbly. By the time the omission was realised the last bottle available had been emptied. The wine had run out and Jack, having realised this sad truth, went down to the bar and bought a bottle of wine for us to take away with us on our honeymoon.

Our wedding present from the Spurway family was a week in a small hotel in Paignton, and, a little later, a 1932 Morris Oxford car which we named Boko. This ancient car was being worked on by Jack and the mechanics who worked for him at his current business venture, Peamore Garage. Velossopop was sadly now redundant. We were sent off to Paignton for our honeymoon in a taxi. The weather was perfect; it was an Indian Summer. The sun was hot and late holiday makers were bathing on Paignton beach. With only a few pounds in our pockets we could not afford to do much more than watch others in envy and begin to realise that our problems may just be beginning. It didn't matter! We were together to face the future and our happiness was complete.

A Time to Sow and a Time to Reap

As newly weds, together with another present, a Jack Russell puppy called Puffles, we arrived at our first home to find water pouring out the front door. A shout from inside the Mill House invited us in. Splashing through ankle deep water in the front hall and through into the kitchen, we were horrified to see Sir John kneeling with his hands extended painfully beneath the kitchen sink clasping a rag around a fractured water pipe.

"Phone for the plumber Michael," he commanded desperately. "I came down to make sure that everything was ready for you and this is what I found. I can't leave it or the water will gush out again." While the farm manager and his new bride were together in their first home, already there were problems and there was work to be done! The torrent of water from the burst water pipe caused an already damp cottage to feel even colder and, for a newly wed couple, inhospitable. Sir John's allowance of coal and logs from the farm soon began to cheer our spirits and dry out the air. We had very little furniture but our generous collection of wedding presents meant that we had all that we needed to begin our united lives.

Valerie had already achieved many things in her life. She had served in the Women's Royal Naval Service and she was a competitive skier, almost making the British Olympic team. Her athletic abilities also extended to fencing at which she was very skilled, and yet she had also worked for her father as a secretary at Peamore Garage, their business near Exeter. However, Valerie's early years had not included the training that would have helped her with the basic skills needed by a housewife. Even so, Valerie began to make our house feel like home.

One morning Sir John arrived at Mill Cottage. The last time he had visited Mill House water had been gushing out through the front door. This time smoke was billowing out of the door. "Michael! Valerie!" Sir John called out in alarm. "The house is on fire." Valerie, distracted for a few moments, had forgotten to watch the breakfast toast under the grill. It had burst into flames and filled the house with acrid smoke, as foul as only burned toast can make it. This could happen to anyone but it was all too much for the young farmer's wife who dissolved into a flood of tears. Seeing that it was all in hand, and that his farm cottage was not likely to be burned to the ground, Sir John tactfully returned to the safety of his Jaguar Mark VI sports car.

Valerie quickly became an excellent, though unpaid, full time member of the farm team. She was put in charge of a new enterprise, a poultry department. This included raising five hundred day old chicks through each stage of their lives, and managing them when they were ready to enter the battery cages which had been installed in the Mill Barn. This was a full time job and at times a difficult and grubby assignment.

We had converted a warm and cosy farm shed, formerly used for calf rearing, into a chick raising room. Day old chicks are very delicate. A large hood containing a specially made infra-red light hung over the central area of the chick pen. The chicks were a delightful sight to see and hear as they dashed in and out of the warmth, peeping as they went. Their lives during the first few weeks were dependent upon the warmth of the glowing lamp which hung above them. To them, this was a god-like source of life. One day the heater failed. Valerie, who nursed her chicks with the greatest care, was horrified to see the distress being shown and vocalised among the chicks. Already some were being squashed and killed as they huddled together trying to keep warm. Decisive action was required. Valerie ran home to fetch a screwdriver thinking that a fuse might have blown or the lamp might have become loose in its socket. In trying to discover the cause she must have touched the screw driver, which was not insulated, against a live wire.

I returned home for our usual morning break at eleven and thought it unusual that Valerie was not at home. Wondering where she was I made my way to the chick house. To my horror I discovered her slumped beneath the now cold lamp, unconscious. The little chicks were sitting all over her body trying to derive warmth from her body as though she was their mother hen. I thought that she must be dead as there was no sign of life. With no response to my efforts to rouse her, I decided to ring 999 for emergency help. Before leaving her I bent over and gave her a kiss. To my relief and joy she stirred, opened her eyes and muttered in astonishment, "What's going on?" She had no burns or other apparent damage but had no recall of how she had got to the chick shed or what had happened.

Our thoughts turned to the dying chicks, and after switching off the electric current at the mains we discovered a poor connection and made the repair. Soon the chicks were experiencing the elation of revival. Thankfully, neither Valerie nor too many chicks suffered lasting damage. I needed some time to overcome the shock which I had experienced. I had really believed that she was dead.

The practice of keeping laying hens in cages has come to be regarded as cruelty to animals. Today we feel that it is wrong to keep hens in such small and unfriendly boxes although at the time the noise and even excitement in the battery house gave the impression that the birds were not conscious of their predicament, and were even excited and reasonably happy.

The ongoing life of the farm brought constant interest and many challenges. Another challenge involved calving. Cows could usually achieve the birth of their offspring alone. However, the dairy herd often had emergencies associated with difficult calvings that would need the farmer's intervention. The birth of animals is just as awe inspiring as that of humans. As a cow gives birth the calf separates from its mother, the umbilical cord snaps and closes completely unaided. To witness this happening is to see one of nature's greatest miracles.

A farmer has to be master of many skills. Many of the most important needs cannot be learned. Over the years, it is as if a gift has been granted. This gift brings one closer to, and helps generate harmony with, nature. The Creator anoints the farmer with wisdom and pastoral gifts which enable him to discern sickness in a young calf, before it is apparent that anything is amiss; or to have a feeling for the right moment to begin a major operation such as ploughing, spring seeding, making hay, or harvesting. Those who farm are usually unaware that they have become the recipients of this gift. While it is not always easy to tell whether a person possesses farming charisma, it is quite evident when it is lacking.

A farmer's day began at five o'clock in the morning and lasted until long after dark. As farm machinery evolved over the years work in the fields could continue later under the strong headlights of the well equipped tractors. In addition to these hours, each season had its own stresses. Tasks ranged from preparing the ground for the sowing of grass seeds, or spring barley or wheat, the making of silage, and the general maintenance of farm roads, gates, hedges, buildings, and machinery. Together these tasks filled the years with work. It was, and still is, a lifestyle which is highly demanding, but abounding in job satisfaction.

One example of the satisfaction of farm work was the art of making silage. When the grass is mown, it is left to slightly wither. Remarkable buck rakes were then mounted on the hydraulic lift arms on the back of the tractor. The grass would then be loaded on the rake as the driver reversed along the mown swards of grasses and clovers. When loaded, and lifted, the tractor, which had heavy weights on the front wheels in order to prevent them from rising, carried the grass into huge pits in the ground to cure until it is needed for fodder in the winter.

The grass was compressed in these pits by the constant action of the tractor tyres driving to and fro.

By winter, if well made, the grass would become a sweet smelling and highly nutritious fodder which the cattle would consume with great relish. Well made silage would fill the farm and countryside with the distinctive fragrance. Badly made silage could be smelt for miles around! The making of good silage required a feel for the job—the gift—and was very rewarding.

In the climate of the Cotswolds, silage making was a more satisfactory method of preserving grass than haymaking. However, a fine summer's day would bring out the mowing machines and haymaking machinery too.

Then I met farmer Nigel Anstee, a tenant farmer on Lord Bathurst's neighbouring Manor Farm. Amidst all these farming activities a friendship with him generated the beginning of a change in my cerebration. I began to experience an awareness of new thoughts and ideas. I didn't know then where it was leading me, but it was, I believe, a spiritual or meditative time of growing up. Much later in life I realised that even at this premature stage I had begun to lift and offer my work up to a higher authority for approval, to ask for a blessing on my newly sown seeds, and when the time came to reap the rewards to give thanks for fruitful harvest.

The modern farming methods at Perrotts Brook were in direct contrast with the traditional yeoman farming of our neighbour. While Perrots Brook benefited from the use of expensive farming equipment, Nigel Anstee methods were still intensive in the use of horses. The difference between the two farms evidenced itself when I observed the peace and quiet and the lack of rush and frenetic activity across the Cotswold stone walls which separated the two of us.

Sunday, in the opinion of Mr. Anstee, was the Lord's Day. If Sunday dawned dry and fine following a week in which the days had been wet and windy, there would be no action over on Manor Farm. This held true even during the peak periods of farm activity, such as haymaking, harvest, sowing or reaping. In contrast, on Perrotts Brook farm the tractors, workers, the manager and his wife would all be hard at work. Sir John and his family would often be at work alongside us helping to speed harvest. But these were enjoyable and exciting days.

On the Lord's Day, across the farm boundary wall, the Anstee family would make their way to the beautiful parish church of All Saints in North Cerney. Here they would join the small and devout congregation who assembled under the loving care of their Rector, the Reverend James Turner. After church, Farmer Anstee would take a leisurely and prayerful walk across his well farmed and attractive acres. I can see him now standing with his hands on his hips looking across the wall, as our busy, busy tractors raced too and fro.

One Sunday I made my way to meet him. His eyes twinkled and he smiled kindly. "It's a grand day!" I greeted him.

"Yes," he agreed. "It's a beautiful fine day and you and your men should be out enjoying it."

"We've got work to do," I replied. "The forecast's bad for tomorrow and we can get all this in the barn tonight."

"I'm not a betting man," he said, "but I'll tell you this—we'll have finished first by the end of the season. You wait and see. This is the Lord's Day and not a working day. It's a day of rest and if you keep His day and turn to Him and trust Him, you'll not suffer for it."

"Well that's your tradition," I responded. And then, as an excuse, "Sir John would rather see us all at work and things done."

The eyes still twinkled. "Let's see who finishes harvest first," he challenged.

As the year continued on its course, a stormy autumn followed. Our expensive modern machinery constantly broke down and the last of the harvest proved difficult to gather. Working seven days a week we had all become tired and the normal spirit of goodwill diminished between the hard working members of our team. I became resentful, that as a manager, I received a fixed weekly wage, but my staff, now earning overtime, had much larger pay packets than I. The joy of seeing hard work bringing good results receded.

Across the wall, the Anstee team of trusted farm workers toiled hard except on Sundays. On a late autumn Sunday, I saw farmer Anstee standing, hands on hips as before, observing us as we struggled to rescue the final loads from the wet and muddy hill sides of Perrotts Brook. We greeted one another. His eyes were alight and kind; there was no trace of triumph. "Still at it then?" he asked, as he watched the tractors rounding up the last bales of straw. I conceded that he had won the day.

Invitations to join his family for Sunday lunch or tea cemented our friendship. A Cotswold farmhouse tea is rather more interesting that an English afternoon tea. This tea was comprised of a cooked meal and Mrs. Anstee was an expert at preparing it.

The example shown to me by this Christian man and his family confirmed the change that was taking place in my heart and mind. Within a few years this change would mature a lead to momentous events in my life.

A Farm of Our Own

I felt as if I had reached the top rung of the farming ladder. I had become an experienced farm manager. I was a married man and very much in love with Valerie. I had overcome the lack of self confidence and shyness that has assailed me throughout my childhood and teenage years. Yet we were concerned that we had not been able to present our parents with a longed for grandchild. We needed children in order to keep the balance in our lives which were dominated by animals. Our two legged 'children', Nellie the sheepdog and Puffles the Jack Russell terrier, were great companions. Nellie was a cross between a Collie, which are noted for their excellence in herding sheep, and a Greyhound. She had inherited the instinct to round up sheep from one parent and a great turn of speed from the other. She had come to us when Nigel Anstee, had rescued her from a cruel owner. He suggested that a sheep dog would be of great value to me. Poor Nellie was a skeleton on legs and of a highly nervous disposition. We pitied the poor creature and so she became a second canine member of the family.

A few days after acquiring Nellie, a number of young chickens had escaped from the ark (a movable chicken pen) in which they were penned. It was towards evening and growing dark. However hard we tried we could not catch all the long legged chicks or coax them back into their safe home. Some nervous chicks flew up into a tree whilst others scattered far and wide across the meadow.

We knew that there were hungry foxes all around. They were sure to have chicken for dinner that night unless we could bring them into the safety of their pens. At that moment Nellie took a hand in the affair. We wondered what she was doing at first. Did she hope for a meal of chicken for herself? Then we realised that she was helping by rounding them up as if they were lost sheep. She was being a hen dog! Very gently and slowly she was using her instinctive ability to guide the chickens to their home.

I discovered that she could round up the Jersey cows too, without causing them to panic. A few weeks later, Sir John suggested that we add a small flock of sheep to our family on the farm. Nellie was over the moon! She took her official position as sheepdog to heart. She gained a lot of self confidence in her role. Nigel Anstee felt that I needed training too, and under his guidance I soon

learned how to control Nellie using hand signals and whistles. She had completely regained her trust in the human race and I had gained a faithful friend.
We also realised that in addition to watching over the cows, sheep and hens, she
was constantly on guard over us and our home. Until she died, was never far
away from my heel and was always ready for action.

Puff, the terrier, was overawed by her talented companion. She came into her
own when luckless rats began to inhabit the corn store. Nellie would chase a rat
out of hiding and Puff would catch, shake and kill the unfortunate rodent.
Working together they made a talented team.

We reached our third harvest at Perrotts Brook. One evening we were loading
bales of straw onto an elevator to lift them to the top of the barn. There men were
building them into neat stacks of straw forty feet or more above our heads. A bale
of straw, having reached the top of the elevator, rolled over the side of the guide
rail. It tumbled downwards and, on reaching the ground, bounced towards me.
Before I could jump out of its path the bale collided with my leg, dislocating the
knee that I had injured whilst playing cricket years before. The aggravated injury
took a long time to heal. My knee never did recover completely and it became a
handicap for the remainder of my life.

During a period of recuperation, I was unable to work. During this time Sir
John appointed an Acting Manager to take my place on the farm. Soon after I
returned to work we faced a major challenge. Valerie's father, whose nickname in
his younger days had been 'mad Jack', had recently overcome a personal business
set back that had almost ended in bankruptcy. The Labour Government, led by
Prime Minister Harold Wilson, had created a massive project intended to assist
the economy of Kenya by encouraging the farming of groundnuts, or peanuts as
they are more commonly known.

Jack, who had built up a new venture in the form a major garage complete
with repair shops, fuel sales and even a café, had won a contract to supply a fleet
of heavy duty lorries to provide transport for the produce of this great humanitar-
ian project. A trusted partner, who had flown over to Nairobi to supervise the
arrival of the lorries and deliver them to the Groundnut Scheme, had failed to
respond to telephone calls or correspondence and appeared to be missing. Jack
had flown out to see what was going on. On arrival in Nairobi he found only the
remains of his fleet of lorries. They had been stripped of their wheels and anything else that could be removed from them. He was unable to trace the missing
partner who had vanished. With him had gone the cheque which had been paid
by the Government as full payment for the vehicles. Jack left in a state of near
bankruptcy and was only saved by a timely loan from his mother.

Following this disaster Jack had fought back gallantly. He rebuilt his resources through the development of a new business. Although at an age when most people would be thinking of taking things a little more easily, working side by side with his wife Audrey, Jack created another new business.

The seaside village of Dawlish Warren, located on the estuary of the River Exe in Devonshire, was growing into an attractive and popular tourist resort. They bought a small piece of derelict land and built a shack. It was almost right on the beach. There they began to sell ice creams, children's buckets and spades, post-cards and notelets. Successfully applying for a licence to become a sub-Post Office, they saw their little business prosper. Within a few years they had been able to build a shop, with living accommodations overhead. It was a wonderful achievement.

Having built up a business with a future, they found that they did not really relish the idea of maintaining the long hours it needed to succeed. The business demanded hard work managing and servicing it. The two loving parents hatched up an astonishingly generous idea that involved selling the business.

One evening the phone rang. Dad Spurway was on the line. "I've been thinking, Mike," he said, his voice rising in pitch with excitement, "wouldn't it be great if we could all get together, form a partnership and buy a small farm?"

My reaction was cautious. I had a secure job at Perrotts Brook. My knee was unreliable. It would often swell up and become very inflamed after trudging up and down the steep slopes of the Cotswolds. In addition we were happy and independent. I was able to delegate the hard work to the farm staff and I was under no pressure to leave. We faced a difficult decision. Every young farmer who is worth anything cherishes a longing that one day he will be master of his own farm. The ambition of achieving this goal had always been in my mind. Suddenly we were faced with the reality of achieving my ambition by becoming proud owners of a half share in a farm which would one day be our own.

I sought advice from those around me. Sir John and Lady Langman were very supportive, but assured us that they did not want us to leave. Affectionately they offered the advice that to take on a small farm, with limited capital, would entail a very real risk. They reminded me that I would not have a team of excellent workers to rely on if my knee, or indeed my general health, was under stress.

Nigel Anstee stood in the midst of his beloved Manor Farm, of which he was not the owner but the tenant of Lord Bathurst. "You know, Michael" he counselled, "We cannot always expect to be safe and secure in this life. Sometimes we are offered a chance to realise our dreams." Valerie had the enhanced anxiety of wondering if we, as daughter and son-in-law, would be able to get along alright with her parents.

One evening Jack telephoned again asking if we could come down. "I think I've found just the place," he said. He sounded excited. "Why not come down and see what you think, old boy?"

Thorn Farm

We made our way down to Devonshire in a pensive mood. We knew that this might be a decisive day—one of those cross roads that occur from time to time during one's life. A day when risks might be taken and the course of our lives changed. We were right.

The Devonshire countryside was looking at its best and as we made our way from Exeter along the valley of the Teign River. We could see the eastern edge of Dartmoor rising from the lush valley farms towards the desolation of Dartmoor.

We were map reading our way toward 'Heltor', Dartmoor's most easterly Tor, or outcropping of granite rock. So far all we knew was that the farm was situated on marginal land, that the farm house stood at 800 feet above sea level and that Heltor was the highest point on the property. Soon we could see the rock high on the hills ahead, emerging from the mist like some huge dinosaur's head surveying the land below. To reach it we had to climb the steep gradient from the valley floor. The climb from the Teign valley to the village of Bridford is steep and winding, containing many blind corners. The Austin van smelt hot and its engine laboured. A lorry transporting the day's collection of milk from the local farms gave us a scare as it appeared around the final bend before we reached the village.

Bridford, a rather motley collection of modern and older cottages, looked drear and uninteresting in comparison with the beautiful villages of the valley. As we drove out of the village the onset of the moorland became more apparent. Outcrops of rock could be seen in the pastures and the farming became decidedly less affluent in character when compared to the farms in the valley. Passing a small bungalow we reached the right hand turn that was to take us down the lane to Thorn Farm. We had arrived at the place that would soon become our home and our living.

The lane led down through a heavy tunnel of branches to a steep unpaved drive and to a lonely looking farm house. As I stood in the farm yard for the first time I experienced a strange feeling of emotion. I felt as if I had arrived home from a long journey. Valerie and I joined hands and just let the silence of the empty sheds and unfarmed fields around us invade our senses. As we recovered from that initial moment of revelation, we became conscious of the realities.

The yard was occupied by a huge pile of manure which filled the whole area and rose to about twelve feet at its highest point. In order to reach the back door of the house, to which we had the key, we had to pick our way around the edge of this foul smelling muck. It was a reminder that until only a few days ago, the Matthews family had been at work, making their living on this near derelict parcel of marginal land on the edge of Dartmoor.

Jack and Audrey arrived and together we viewed the farm. The house was far from being a traditional Devonshire long house, those beautiful farm houses, with thatched roofs and roses growing round the doors. Thorn Farm was a practical square dwelling, but set amidst stunning scenery.

The kitchen, living rooms and bedrooms were ordinary, but the views from the windows were most pleasant. As we gazed upwards across the 115 acres of farm land it seemed to be calling me out to inspect its territory. We took a stiff climb up a farm track which led to Heltor. Scrambling to the summit of the rock we could view the whole place and see right across the Devon valleys to that other great area of desolation to the west, Exmoor.

Here was a massive challenge to a would-be farm owner. I had no illusions that it would be easy to make a living on such a marginal farm, but one's heart rules one's head when you fall in love, and Valerie and I had fallen in love with this chunk of old England. As I looked at dear old Jack I could tell that he too was having an emotional experience. Had he also felt the insistence of the farm to take it in, I wondered? Watching him I felt that he had already become bonded with the place.

Being a practical man who had once managed Tea Estates in Ceylon, I could see that he was already mapping out the improvements that would transform the house and take a water supply out to the fields nearby. Audrey was in the house poking about the ancient Rayburn kitchen stove, sensing that her role might well be that of mother and housewife, a role that she already filled with great success.

"Well Mike," Jack said with the broadest of grins on his face, "What do you think?"

I felt Valerie's hand in mine; it tightened slightly as she waited for my answer. "Yes," I said, "It's just the place." It was early spring in the year 1956.

Back at Perrotts Brook Farm we faced the difficult task of informing the Langman's and the farm staff that we had decided to take on Thorn Farm. Everyone was very supportive, but their fears for us were very evident. We were aware that we were setting out on a journey into the unknown and leaving the love, friendship and security with which we had been blessed for the past few years.

The business of buying Thorn Farm and receiving the title deeds was executed surprisingly quickly. I was now the proud owner of a half share in this 115 acre farm. Since the farm house was vacant we could move in as soon as we wished.

My first task was to consider the initial stocking of the farm. We would need some first class dairy cows. The previous owner had left a milking bail, milking machines and equipment in good condition and ready for use. Meanwhile Farmer Spurway went in search of a farm tractor and equipment.

John Hebditch, whose herd of Ayrshire dairy cows I knew well from the days when I worked for him, was excited to hear the news that we had bought a farm in Devonshire. "I've got some first class 'in-calf' heifers ready for you," he said. "Why not come down and pick some out? They'll do well down there."

Valerie's dad announced that he'd bought a tractor. It would be delivered that very day. I was now used to modern equipment. Sir John Langman's ability to buy the very latest Fordson and Ferguson tractors had spoilt me. I had even been using the then innovative hydraulic lift equipment, which was causing a revolution on the farms in Britain. This would be no more!

I was therefore unprepared for the sight of a very dilapidated truck which appeared in the farm yard. On the back was a battered Fordson Standard tractor, like the ones that had arrived in Britain during the 1939 war as part of the Marshall Aid from the United States. I had first driven a Fordson Standard way back in the 1940s.

I tried to conceal my feelings. I knew that we would need a much better machine than that if we were to be able to cope with the very steep slopes on the farm, let alone make hay and silage during our first summer. We would have to manage somehow!

Farm sales were always a great outing which provided the occasion to meet one's new neighbours and purchase used but efficient equipment at very low prices. At these sales we purchased equipment that my old time tractor could haul. Our newly acquired accessories were all items that would have been disposed of at Perrotts Brook long ago.

I soon discovered that our tractor had one serious fault. She had a cracked seat which, when negotiating rough ground, would very painfully grab the rear anatomy of the driver. Shouts induced by severe pain could often be heard echoing across fields. 'Nippit', as she became known, got to work on clearing massive rocks from pastures which were being prepared for reseeding. The ancient tractor surprised us and fulfilled her purpose during our first two years. We all had to agree that she turned out to be a darned good buy.

The time came to accept John Hebditch's offer. When we arrived at Newcross Farm the cattle were penned in the yard. "Now, it's up to you Michael. You can have the first pick and I'll keep the rest. £80 a piece to you. That's fair enough isn't it?" John Hebditch was being very generous. I knew that these same heifers would cost me £100 each in the market. I agreed to the price. I could afford five. But in calf heifers would not produce enough milk to keep a family of four, and so John generously thought for a few moments. "What you need is a good old timer to fill up the milk churns for you." Seeing one of the mature and highly productive cows in his herd coming by on her way in for milking, John inquired "Do you remember old Broadhorn? I think she was born when you were here. How about having her in the deal too? She'll be a good leader for the others and she's got a lot of life left in her yet."

Broadhorn was given as a discount on the five young animals. The foundation for our Thorn Farm herd of Ayrshire cows was formed. Within five years they were to win the trophy for being the highest yielding herd for a small farm in the county of Devonshire. Years later, John admitted ruefully that I had chosen his five best animals on that memorable day.

Before the cattle could be transported I needed time to survey the farm and to check and mend the farm gates as necessary. The hedges, too, needed fencing in many places otherwise it was likely that the excited new arrivals might abscond quickly into the neighbouring farms. Such escapades would not endear us to our new neighbours. As they were all 'tuberculin tested' (certified to be free of tuberculosis), a benefit that secured a higher price for the milk produced, a perimeter fence had to be erected alongside the boundaries where they might fraternise with their cousins on neighbouring Heltor Farm. To keep this certification, a gap of at least ten feet had to be maintained between the farms.

Before we set to work on the farm, Audrey and Valerie decreed that the floors of the farm house, being ingrained with the dirt of the past, needed scrubbing. While dad Spurway began the task of mending gates and fences, I set to work on my knees with bucket and scrubbing brush. The weather had turned extremely cold and there was little heating in the house. Two days later I became very ill. My chest was heavy and I had developed a wrenching cough. Then the worst happened. A burning fever caused me to become delirious. I felt as if I was bound with heavy chains and I was fighting for every breath. A call to Dr. Glyn Jones, the Doctor in Moretonhampstead, the nearest small town, brought a helpful and speedy response. After a thorough examination he announced that I should be admitted to hospital. I had pneumonia.

Prescribing penicillin, a drug which was only just beginning to be circulated for general use, Doctor Jones counselled warmth and rest for his patient. The unscrubbed floors would have to stay dirty for a while.

Three weeks later, after an illness which I learned later had at one point been life threatening, I was declared fit to undertake light work. I quickly gained strength. Soon the floors were clean, the fences mended and the hedgerows secured. The time had arrived for the cattle lorry to transport the six founding members of our herd to their new home.

On the appointed day the chosen six arrived. They were let loose to have a free run of much of the farm. When I offered payment to John he declined my cheque. "Not yet," he said. "Take a little time to get established and pay me when you are ready."

The Thorn Farm herd took off into their exciting tree, gorse and bracken wilderness. They mooed greetings to the cattle and sheep in the fields around them. In return they received some welcoming bellows and bleats from the well established herds and flocks of our neighbours. Nellie the sheepdog, who had no doubt been wondering why she had no work to do of late, hunted boldly around her new charges, obviously proud and glad to be back at work. Broadhorn provided us with our first home produced milk that evening. Production had begun.

The following morning Nellie and I set out to find and say good morning to the herd. Nellie had already located where they were but, to my immense concern, there was one missing. Nellie began to search. Down at the furthest point possible from the farm house she lay down, her head pointing towards some impenetrable bushes. Hurrying towards here I saw that she was wagging her tail with delight. Garnet, one of the five pregnant cows, had presented us with our first new born calf.

At 8 o'clock in the morning the milk lorry arrived at the top of our farm lane to collect our consignment of pure, clean Ayrshire milk. Broadhorn had produced eight gallons of steaming and fulsome milk all by herself. Our herd had already increased. Now we had seven.

A Time for Pride and Joy

I ran home to tell the family the great news that our first calf had been born. The happy event had the effect of validating our undertaking and our determination to transform this barren farm into a land flowing with milk. Perhaps the honey would come later!

We all crowded around the new arrival over which Garnet was mooing and fussing whilst Nellie, who was always nearby, kept a tactful distance. I gathered the new born calf into my arms and hoisting her onto my shoulders called Garnet to follow me back to the safety of a freshly strawed calving shed. There can be few more lovely sights than a cow nursing her first born. The calf can stagger onto its spindly legs astonishingly quickly and within moments find its way to the supply of warm, nourishing baby food that at once sends its strength into its body. We now had two cows in production and, pint by pint, our meagre income began to accrue.

This was a time for birthdays on the farm. Valerie and I had longed that we might ourselves have been blessed with the coming of a child. The days at work were long and hard. Our venture would demand our personal attention for the many years that lay ahead. But what, we began to wonder, was the point of all our planning, all the long hours of hard and heavy work, if in the end we had no heir to inherit the farm? Since no child, as yet, had come into our family we sought medical advice and took measures to try to enhance fertility. As it turned out, we were equally afflicted with various impediments to conception and we were told that a joyful moment of creation was unlikely to occur.

One day during a visit to Dr. Jackson, the specialist doctor who was advising us, she asked "Have you two ever thought about the possibility of adopting a baby?" The idea was previously suggested by Valerie, but at that time I had not been very encouraging in my response. Neither of us had experienced any contact with parents who had adopted children. Dr. Jackson was not so reticent. She informed us that she supervised a small private adoption agency and that it we would like to think about it she would undoubtedly be able to find a child for us. While our parents had never even mentioned the subject of our childless marriage, we sensed that they were waiting discreetly and patiently, hoping for a grandchild.

The five 'Newcross girls', as we called the precious in-calf heifers, all gave birth to their calves. Even Mrs. Spot, the Wessex saddleback sow that had joined the growing family of animals, gave birth to a litter of eight piglets. We could not ignore the fact that the farm was missing a little human person who would grow up there and perhaps one day become its proud owner.

One evening we were tucked up in bed with the sounds of the farm—the gentle lowing of the cows out at pasture and the chickens, perhaps startled by something moving within the safety of their hen house, cackling neurotically. Suddenly utter quietness, peace and tranquillity enveloped the house and the living farm that surrounded it. In that instant we made the decision to pursue adoption. We would telephone Doctor Jackson in the morning.

When we woke up that morning, I crept out early to call the cows in for milking. There is something special about the early hours of the day on the farm. When the new day dawns it feels as if nothing has happened that has spoilt the natural world, as if life begins anew. Every morning presents the opportunity for that new start.

Milking time was always a time for thought, even meditation. Although I had never been a church goer, I would often feel that I was in contact with something, or could it have been someone, within and beyond myself with whom I could commune. I knew that I would have to be decisive when I saw Valerie at breakfast time. Would adoption work? Could we afford to take on a child? We need every penny that we earn in order to develop the farm, I reasoned with myself. My love for Valerie was so great and I knew that she was excited with the possibility, that despite everything, we would be able to have a baby.

After breakfast, in that rather sleepy period during which I would think of returning to the farm work, there was a period of silence. I knew that Valerie did not wish to push me into decision. "Well," I said cheerfully, "I'd better get back to work and you might as well ring Dr. Jackson! What shall we have, a boy or a girl?" We agreed that as we would not have that choice if we were the natural parents, we would simply put our faith in the doctor and wait and see. Within days a telephone call from Dr. Jackson informed us that she knew of a young woman who had reluctantly decided that she would have to offer her, as yet unborn, child for adoption.

The days and weeks passed without further news until one morning Valerie ran out to find me on the farm. I'd never seen her so vibrantly happy. The child had been born. It was a lovely little boy. He would like to come to his mummy and daddy in about three weeks' time. A natural parent has nine months to make preparations. We had three weeks to prepare, milk the cows, run the farm and learn about babies.

During the same period developments had taken place within our happily working partnership. Jack and Audrey sensed that with the advent of a potential grandson the house would not be large enough to accommodate a nursery and them. With the satisfaction that they had successfully laid the foundation for our future at Thorn Farm, Jack and Audrey suggested that I should approach the bank to see if they might be willing to refinance the venture in favour of Valerie and me. They felt Valerie and I were ready to go forward with the venture independently.

Jack had found a new opportunity for him too. He had seen a pub at Shobrooke near Crediton. He could become the tenant by taking on the lease. There was an empty coach house nearby, in the grounds of a now vanished stately home in Shobrooke Park, which he could buy extremely inexpensively and make into a pleasant residence. We owed him a tremendous debt of gratitude for enabling us to get the farm established, but now it was time for us to go our separate ways. Sharing a house has great compensations but with the generation gap, the closeness of family and coupled with the loss of privacy, there were times that caused us all to feel stress.

The future would depend on whether I would be able to convince the bank that the farm was well enough established to qualify for a loan that would enable us to become the sole owners. The manager of Martins Bank in Exeter, Mr. Crossley, agreed to come and look over the farm. Everything would depend on the banks decision to lend us £10,000. Anxiously we guided Mr. Crossley from barn to milking shed, well aware that all were in great need of modernisation.

The meadows, where only bracken and coarse grass had grown before, were now looking green and productive. Nippit had helped clear the rocks, contractors had come in to plough, and grass seed mixtures had been sown. The meadow with the steepest slope on the farm had been re-sown and the Ayrshire herd were standing in formation from the top to bottom of the electric fence as we strip grazed the lush green grass. The cows looked in the peak of condition. The cheques engendered by their milk production had sustained our ascetic way of life and enabled us to reclaim much of this very marginal land. Mr. Crossley was one of the last of an ancient species of bank managers. Although coming from the north of England, he knew the problems of a farmer on land such as this. Returning to the comfort of the homestead and refreshed with a cup of tea he concurred we had a tough task ahead of us. But he informed us that in his opinion our progress so far persuaded him that we were worth backing. We could now reach the summit of the farming ladder—sole ownership of a farm. Now we had to be strong and resolute in order for our farming business to survive and, with good fortune, to prosper.

Farm incomes on the uplands were low and not giving a fair return to the hard working families who lived in these less productive areas. While this was known to us as we ventured into independent farm ownership, unexpected help was at hand. The Nuffield Foundation sponsored a programme to finance the testing of new ideas that may help these farms. Two men had put Thorn Farm on the list of selected farms in the district. Some of these farms were run by well established Devonshire farmers while others, like ours, represented farmers who had not been born to farming but were making an attempt to establish themselves. One of these men was Alan Ford, the Area Secretary of the National Farmers Union and whose encouragement and advice had been greatly valued in the past. The other was Mr. John Baglow, the Area Officer of the Agricultural Advisory Service in Exeter, who had been following our enterprise and renewing our hope whenever we became overwhelmed with weariness.

My first tractor, Nippit, was still at work on the farm when needed, but now I had a modern Ferguson tractor. This was a great improvement. I had reclaimed and established excellent grassland on some of the steepest slopes. I wondered what else the Nuffield Foundation programme would do for us, apart from carrying on the process.

Jack, a great innovator, had fixed up an antique ship's telephone, which he had found at an Army and Navy surplus store. This phone would give out a frightening series of whoops when the caller in the kitchen cranked at the handle at sufficient speed. The telephone connected with the high level milking parlour, which we had now built, and, with cables that ran along the hedgerows, to Heltor Barn. The barn stood in one of the more distant fields and was the store for all the hay and straw bales, as well as being a great centre for the sheep at lambing time.

The peace and quiet of milking time was rudely disturbed by the whooping of the phone. The bucket type milking machines of the time would sound like a heart beat and the rhythmic sound coupled with the sound of milk tumbling into the buckets could bring a soporific feeling into the hearts of both man and beast. Alarmed, Ragtag, one of the original five 'Newcross Maidens', gave an almighty kick and swept the milking machines off her very productive teats. Precious milk flowed out of the rubber connecting tubes and ran down the gutter to waste.

Valerie was calling from the kitchen. "There's a chap called Derek Smith who says he's from BBC Television on the phone," she said excitedly. "He says that he wants to come out here with his film unit on Tuesday. He's making a documentary about the Nuffield Project. What shall I say?"

There was no time to dally. Chaos can soon reign when milking cows get upset and their restlessness gave warning of a more industrial action if I did not restore order quickly. "Tell him that's OK," I shouted.

Valerie insists that she added, "He's coming for two or three days." But I had hung up the phone. Ragtag looked guiltily at the spilt milk as if to say 'Did I cause all that trouble?' Not long after this incident I installed a radio in the parlour. The soothing sound of waltzes proved to be the most popular music while the clamour of the current rock and roll was certainly not to the milking herds taste.

Later that morning as we were having breakfast, the telephone rang again. Valerie turned quite pale as she listened. She thoughtfully concluded the call with the words "Yes, Doctor Jackson, that will be just fine. We'll collect him on Tuesday." Our adopted son would be joining us on Tuesday as well!

The preparations for the little boy's arrival absorbed all the help that would have usually been available on the farm. The thought of BBC cameras showing the entire farming population our farm filled me with dismay. The advent of summer meant long hours of cutting and gathering grass for silage as well as preparations for haymaking. Although I had been trained to keep my dairy farm clean and tidy, this rush of work caused some of the routine work to be delayed. Needless to say the farm was not as presentable as I would have liked it to be.

At such a time old and trusted friends can be an invaluable asset. Ann Bundle, who had been Valerie's best friend since they had served in the Women's Royal Naval Service together and was an experienced mother, responded to the expectant mother's anxious telephone call for advice. "Darling! I'd better come over. You're going to need some help!" Ann could not, however, be with us for some days.

We had been in to meet our son when he was only five days old. This initial visit had been a case of love at first sight. We had reasoned with one another that no child has the opportunity to choose who will be his parents and that adoption was a special vocation. We had such longing to be parents and we knew that his natural mother, for whom we felt great compassion, had decided to offer him for adoption in her love for him. She felt that she could not offer him a secure and happy future on her own.

We found it agonising to think of the heartbreak that must have been in that young mother's heart. We knew that she had struggled over the decision. It can only have been a time of anguish and unimaginable stress for her.

I felt the responsibility of fatherhood very strongly. Valerie's maternal instincts had been apparent from the moment when she first held him in her arms. The look of adoration in her eyes and in the baby's very searching scrutiny of each of us created a wonderful moment of bonding. We felt that he had interviewed and taken us on for the job in hand. We decided to name him Timothy.

Family Time

We had arranged to pick up Timothy and bring him home after we had completed the morning milking. The basic chores of a small dairy farm impose a strict discipline on its owners. Milking time occurs twice a day. The dairy cows, their calves, the chickens, and pigs need to be fed on a regular basis. The persistent trumpet calls of a herd of hungry cows and calves will ensure that they receive immediate attention. The animals could easily become very domineering. That afternoon we were also to experience for the first time the raucous cry of an apparently starving baby demanding to be fed!

After having a joyful reunion with Timothy at the nursing home, and receiving abysmally inadequate counselling concerning his feeding routine and personal needs, we purchased his first supplies of baby food, feeding bottles and all the other paraphernalia that a three week old baby requires

When we arrived home, a Land Rover and a very large truck were negotiating the sharp corner that led into our farm lane. The top of the truck was brushing the overgrown hedgerows that formed a tunnel much of the way down to the farm. We turned in behind the convoy. The British Broadcasting Corporation had timed their arrival to coincide with the exact moment of Timothy's homecoming.

On arrival it was necessary to introduce Timothy to the ancestral pram. A vintage family pram, which had been commandeered by my mother Moo, had arrived from my cousins, 'Beetle' and Tony Nation. This pram had seen service with all the cousins and now was awaiting the heir to Thorn Farm. Timothy was firmly, but gently, tucked up in it while we greeted the BBC crew and distributed the first of a large number of cups of tea or coffee all round. As we introduced our brand new son I thought that he had given his admirers a friendly grin, but the consensus of opinion disagreed. The grin was, they informed me, only a sign that he had indigestion. I still claim that they were mistaken.

Nellie, the sheepdog, was already at work. She had appointed herself as the baby's guardian. To her, Tim was a human lamb which she would protect from any kind of fox, four or two legged. The farms cats, too, were challenged not to come within jumping range of her protégé.

"I'd like to include you personally in the making of our documentary," Derek told me. "We need to show the farm and, if possible, to get you to act out an interview with Martins Bank. Do you think Mr. Crossley would be willing to do that?" A phone call to the bank manager confirmed that Mr. Crossley would be very glad to participate. We began to rehearse for my short but enjoyable experience as a TV actor.

Soon the discordant sounds in the background conveyed the message that Tim, with his allies in the cows, had united in their cause. It was time that they were fed. While Valerie prepared our first offering of refreshment for Tim, I conducted Derek Smith, the film units Producer, around the farm. For once Nellie declined to act as guide and stayed on watch, nose on paws, eyes alert and tail wagging as it had never wagged before.

The dictatorial powers manifested by an always hungry baby, the dairy herd, and the schedule of the film unit, ensured a three day period of intense activity. The film crew were mobilised to assist and proved to be a great workforce. Many hands make light work and the farm work was done quickly so that we could begin the task of filming. Out came the clapper board and before I knew it Derek had called 'Take One'. I was filmed while I was busy at work in the milking parlour.

Moo, whose health had been deteriorating all too quickly in recent years, had been at work with her knitting needles. She had produced, and sent to us, a cuddly matinee jacket for her first grandson, of whom she was obviously very proud. We had equipped ourselves with a book written by an American paediatrician named Dr. Spock. This book had been strongly recommended by Ann Bundle and was acclaimed as being the best guide to parenthood. Full of helpful advice it was constantly a source for reference. However, today's parents and doctors would disagree profoundly with much of its content.

At last, late in the evening, quiet descended on the farm aside from the gentle lowing of the contented herd of Ayrshire cows. The wonderful sight and sounds that proved that Tim's hunger was being assuaged yet again indicated that a strong bond had already been made between mother and child. As I watched, his tiny hands reached out towards me and I suddenly became aware of an awesome fact. In the midst of all the day's intense activity, I had become a father. It was a time of happy excitement.

The making of the documentary film brought new challenges. Derek Smith guided me through the introductory shots whilst we milked the cows together. The herd seemed to sense that they were now Hollywood stars! The glorious scenery that framed our little Devonshire farm created a wonderful backdrop for the story to be told.

I wondered if this in-depth study of a group of traditional and more experimental farms could bring new life to these marginal farm lands of Dartmoor. But I was happy to go along with the process. The visit to see our bank manager, Mr. Crossley, was to be one of the major scenes. After several alarming rehearsals, and camera and voice tests, I was filmed sprucing myself up for my epic journey to Exeter. Under Valerie's ever watchful eye I washed, shaved and donned my only suit, which was many years old having been given to me by my brother Edward for my twenty-first birthday. It seldom came out of the closet! I was to be filmed hurrying down the stairs into the small front hall and out past Tim's pram and into the farm yard. Our dilapidated Austin A40 van would then be seen trundling up the steep incline to the farm lane and disappearing as I made the twelve mile journey into Exeter. After several rehearsals and dummy runs Derek announced that the next time it would be for real. I would be on camera.

A signal from Derek launched me into my great scene. Down the stairs I hurried. The camera was set up a short distance from, and directly in front of, the doorway. I made my way down the stairway and into the front garden. There was a moment of hush and then a gust of hysterical laughter from the BBC crew and the watching family. Derek put his hand on my shoulder kindly and said, "Michael, I think we will have to do that again." I couldn't think what I had done wrong and became a little embarrassed by the laughter. Then I realised the truth. My exit from the house was faithfully recorded on film but I had neglected to check that my trouser fly buttons were fastened. Take Two was more successful.

The bank manager proved to be a natural and accomplished actor. We were filmed facing each other across his desk talking over the farm's prospects and concerning my desperate need for a loan. My request was granted. We signed some imaginary papers together. I had his promises to back Thorn Farm on record! As I left the bank, I heard Derek's voice shouting 'cut'. Two attractive girls had happened to walk past the bank's doors just as I emerged, a fact which had diverted the camera man's attention. The camera had swung away from me to follow their progress down the street. The second take was brightened by their presence.

During the intervals between filming the routine farm work had to be done. Derek and I worked side by side on the farm. These moments were to become of more importance to the future than I realised at the time. As Derek listened to my life story he became pensive. When work was finished for the day we talked long into the night. "Do you and Valerie intend to spend the rest of your lives here?" he asked.

I replied, "I suppose so, unless ..."

In the moment of my hesitation Derek said quietly, "I think there are other things that you could do very well." This was the first time that anyone had suggested that I might have gifts that could be of value other than for my chosen way of life in farming.

"Oh well," I responded, "who knows!" Then I added, "And if we don't get to bed it will soon be time to milk those ... cows again!" The daily duties could never be waived in order to savour time to think or dream.

After the morning milking the BBC convoy went on its way to visit other neighbouring farms. We sadly waived goodbye to Derek and his charming film crew. As we parted Derek said "Well, all the best for the future. I hope that we've been of some help." He added, "But I wouldn't be surprised to hear that you are doing something completely different in a few years time." This was a prophecy that was to come true.

After the BBC film crew had left, Thorn Farm returned to its daily routine. Derek's words receded into the background. We could not envisage anything that would cause us to want to forsake the farm. We put all our strength and skills into making it a success.

The effect of the Nuffield Foundation's project report was the establishment of a 'Machinery Syndicate'. Expensive equipment was supplied by the Foundation in order to initiate a cooperative venture between ourselves and neighbouring farms. A powerful International tractor with an attached Forage Harvester and trailer would be shared between us. This would encourage and speed up the making of silage. Each farm would share the task of operating it so that, in effect, a new partnership was formed in the immediate neighbourhood. We were also encouraged to join together in order to purchase our petrol and oil, and our food stuffs, in order to reduce the costs.

Bulk buying was quite a new experience for me and the other local farmers. The arrangement worked well though. The gathering of winter fodder, and the consequent reduction in our reliance upon expensive bought feeding stuffs, brought about a useful improvement in our financial position. This partnership also developed a great closeness between farmers from such varied backgrounds. Inevitably it was not without problems. But it opened up a new horizon for those who were prepared to accept the necessary changes in their lives.

The local Vicar's visits to the farm had been few and far between. That had not been his fault. On such occasions I would hasten into hiding in a remote part of the farm. However Valerie had been limited to the making of arrangements for the baptism of Timothy. The Vicar of Bridford, the Reverend Cyrill Gray, had kindly assented to the christening of our little son. We duly presented Tim for Holy Baptism in a private ceremony at the Church of St. Thomas á Beckett, Bridford. Our friends and neighbours, Geoff and Betty Baines, with their son Alan were also present.

Attendance in church was always a stressful experience for me. I felt out of place, embarrassed and uneasy. The Church of England service of Holy Baptism, as it was presented in the Book of Common Prayer, is liturgically very moving. The words and actions performed over an innocent child appeared to me to be overwhelming and full of pathos. I wondered how such a little one could be so sinful. Yet the reminder that I, too, had been baptised many years before in the Church at St. Mary, Weybridge in Surrey, intrigued me,

'*Verily, verily, I say unto thee, except a man be born of water and of the Spirit he cannot enter into the Kingdom of God.*' The words from Saint John's Gospel coupled with the question '*Dost thou renounce the devil and all his works, the vain pomp and glory of the world, with all the covetous desires of the same,*' irrelevant as they sounded for our little son, were none the less deposited in my memory and almost certainly my heart at that moment. I was unaware that they had been sown, like seeds, in my own heart many years earlier when I was baptised. I had also been made an heir of an everlasting salvation. Just as the Vicar had received Tim '*into the congregation of Christ's flock and signed him with the sign of the cross, in token that hereafter he shall not be ashamed to confess the faith of Christ crucified, and manfully to fight under his banner, against sin, the world and the devil; and to continue as Christ's faithful soldier and servant until his life's end*' so also had I been prayed for all those years ago at St. Mary's Church.

The Birthday Present

One day Audrey was with us on one of her frequent visits to the farm and said "You never told me that you had got a horse."

Mystified by the remark, Valerie replied "We haven't got one."

"Oh, but I saw a horse in the old stable," she insisted. We all trooped outside to the stable. "Well I'll be blowed," she said, using her favourite expression of surprise. "I could have sworn I saw a horse in there." We were puzzled.

A few weeks later Sir John and Lady Langman came to visit us. They had wanted to come and see how we were getting on and to meet Tim for the first time. As we showed them out into the farm yard, Sir John said "Valerie, do please so us your horse." We looked at him in amazement.

"We haven't got a horse," we insisted for a second time.

"But I saw it," he said, "in the stable. It's a grey mare." On being shown the derelict and empty stable he was incredulous.

Some months later, I met an elderly man who I had never seen before. He wore a tweed cutaway jacket, waistcoat, breeches and a pocket watch on a chain. He was leaning over a gate and gazing down towards the farm house. Interested to know who he was, I strolled over to have a chat.

"I used to farm here at one time," he told me. "Has anyone ever told you about the day of the accident? I had a young grey mare, a working horse, not fully broken. Well one day she tried to jump the old iron fence that used to be down there. It had spikes along the top. She reared up and came down right on top of it. She was impaled by the spikes. Terrible it was. The veterinary had to come and put her down, poor old devil." We chatted for a while and then, bidding me a cheerful and polite farewell, he went off down the hill towards the neighbouring Heltor Farm.

A few days later, one of the men from Bridford village was visiting the farm to do some odd jobs that needed attention for us. I mentioned my meeting with the old timer. He stopped what he was doing and looked at me in some awe. "Did he say what his name was?" he asked.

"No," I answered. I described the old man to him. He looked at me with amazement.

"That was old farmer Roberts you described, and I could take you down to the churchyard and show you his grave. He's been dead for years." We had farm ghosts!

The long and hard hours of manual work which were needed to sustain a small dairy farm in the late 1950's and early 60's precluded the taking of holidays, or even a complete day off. As Tim started to grow older we would occasionally escape from the harsh regime of 'all work and no play' and race down to one of Devonshire's beautiful beaches. After having fun paddling, building sand castles and eating fish and chips, we would have to hasten back to work. We often wondered if the chips were made from our own home grown potatoes. Upon arrival back at the farm, we were always relieved to see the bread winners, who would be standing huddled together behind the sturdy gate into the yard, proclaiming that we were late. They were just bursting to be relieved of their milk.

During this period, Moo finally paid a visit to us. She had come down from her flat in Battersea to meet with her first grandson. Tim and his grandmother spent a few moments gazing at each other. Tim's eyes searched his granny's face with interest, greeting her with delighted squeals and smiles. We wondered what the new granny would think of her adopted grandson. Looking down at the little boy who had come into our lives and who was already bringing us so much joy, she said quietly, "I couldn't have done better myself."

Tim and Moo began a great friendship. Sadly however, her failing health and severe attacks of asthma were taking a steady toll on her. She died shortly thereafter. Her death left another black hole in my life. I realised that through the contacts she acquired during her faithful service at the National Federation of Women's Institutes she had quietly influenced and guided my future. Time and time again she had provided the introductions that led to the vital chances that helped me make my way in the world. I had much to be thankful to her for. But the years after my father's death had been difficult for her, not just with regard to her health. I knew that during this period the family's financial resources must have been draining away. My mother had often expressed the hope that 'one day our ship will come home'. Her ship never did return. She was still hoping for it at the time of her death in 1962 at the age of 66, in St. George's Hospital, Hyde Park Corner, London.

As Tim grew older he showed signs of loving the farm. By the time of his second birthday he was already assisting by helping to assemble the milking machines. Although just a child, he would push his way through the assembled herd of cows on his way to help me in the milking parlour.

One morning as I was at work in the fields, I realised that it was at last really beginning to feel like spring-time. Winter had been an especially hard and arduous season. The last few months had been especially difficult for Valerie who hated cold weather and dreaded the annual fall of snow which always descended on Dartmoor. Thinking that she deserved a treat I suddenly remembered that it would soon be her birthday. I had forgotten to get her a present!

Making an excuse that I had to go into town to fetch some spare parts for the tractor, I hurried into Exeter. As I drove the familiar route I racked my brains to try to think of a suitable gift. Whatever it turned out to be it would be well deserved. The fact that the farm was doing well was due to our working partnership. In addition, she took the greater share of caring for Tim's needs. We had recently taken a half share in a flock of sheep too and Valerie had been sharing the night watch with me at lambing time. She had also mastered the task, which I disliked, of giving the injections that all new born lambs needed in order to protect them from various diseases. What could I find that would reflect my love and appreciation for all that she had been doing?

A barren search of the bigger stores brought no inspiration. The time was passing fast and I would soon have to be on my way back to the farm. Just as I was becoming desperate I noticed a display in the window of Boots, The Chemist. At that time Boots included a bookstall. A placard in the shop window proclaimed 'The Bible as you never read it before'. Remembering that Valerie had been a practicing Christian before our marriage and had sometimes even invited me to join her and her parents in their Sunday visit to their parish church, I decided to investigate further.

The 'New English Bible', I read. 'The Gospels in today's English.' That might just be what I want, I thought. On entering the shop, I saw that the counter selling the books was quite crowded. Shyly, and hoping that no one I knew would be nearby, I made my way to the counter. The book was nicely bound and fairly expensive. This would be a great gift. Having bought some gift wrap I hurried back to the van and made my way home. On arrival I saw that Valerie and Tim had already marshalled the cows into the yard. The soothing sound of the milking machines and the contented munching of the cows who were placidly chewing their cud, informed me that milking was in full swing.

The birthday was not for a few days, so I concealed my gift in the airing cupboard and then joined the busy mother and son who were hard at work. "Did you get what you needed?" Valerie asked. I wondered if she guessed the true reason for my sudden rush to town!

That evening, I wanted to see what this new Bible was like. Concealing it, I smuggled it into the smallest room in the house which was about the only place that would provide me with the privacy I required for my secret reading. I opened the New English Bible at random and read these words:

God loved the world so much that he gave his only Son, that everyone who has faith in him may not die but have eternal life. It was not to judge the world that God sent his Son into the world, but that through him the world might be saved.

I thought of our son, Timothy, for by now we never even thought of him as adopted. He was OUR son. But could we ever put him at risk? Could some other love ever surpass our love for him? I read on.

The man who puts his faith in Him does not come under judgment; but the unbeliever has already been judged in that he has not given his allegiance to God's only son. Here lies the test, the light has come into the world, but men preferred darkness to light because their deeds were evil. Bad men hate the light to avoid it, for fear their practices should be shown up. The honest man comes to the light so that it may be clearly seen that God is in all he does.

My time of privacy could not be extended. Awkward questions would be asked if I stayed longer. Concealing the book once again I returned it to the airing cupboard.

Farming provides plenty of hard manual work but also gives moments of beauty and joy: a wonderful sunrise, a new born calf, a blackbird singing his heart out, a breeze blowing across a field of corn. The next few days brought about a more cerebral time of emotion. I had spent as many minutes as I could continuing to read this best seller. I did not fully understand the meaning of the passages that I had read but they had given me a determination to read on and discover more about the message in this strange book.

The day of the birthday, April 14, dawned. The book was wrapped and ready for presentation. Valerie took it into her hands. "A book?" she remarked. "When am I going to have time to read a book?"

"This is a thriller!" I told her, "As soon as you have unwrapped it, I'd like to borrow it. I started reading it and I couldn't put it down."

Valerie tore open the wrapping and read the title. "The New English Bible," she said in awe, and added "I never thought that you would have bought that for my birthday."

"You can have it later," I said. "I've got a lot of reading to do." The truth was that I was becoming more and more interested in the message of the New Testament, but could not associate it with what I perceived to be the activities of the village church and its leader. It all seemed to be irrelevant to the challenge presented by the exciting stories in the New English Bible.

The Lost Sheep

We began to wonder if we might be able to expand our venture by adding more land to our little kingdom of 115 acres. Small farms were becoming less and less viable and in due time we might even be swallowed up ourselves by a local farmer who was beginning to buy up land as soon as it became available.

By now we had obtained mortgages on over 90% of the value of the farm, In order to save valuable capital, of which we were very short, we decided to approach a retired sheep farmer who had been introduced to us by our friends Geoff Baines and Peter Morris. Mr. Smerdon was keen to enter into a partnership with a young farmer. He would be willing to provide the capital for the purchase of a small flock of sheep—about fifty breeding ewes. In return we would provide the grazing land and care for the sheep. The profit would come from the value of their wool fleeces at shearing time and from the sale of the fat lambs. Mr. Smerdon would pay the veterinary surgeon's account and we would go halves on the profits. The system was known in Devonshire as 'going half-crease'.

This was a meeting of ancient and modern minds. Mr. Smerdon was a traditional sheep farmer and I had little previous experience of shepherding, although John Hebditch had passed on quite a lot of his experience with sheep during my time at Newcross Farm. Looking over the farm and shrewdly assessing whether his sheep would be in safe hands, Mr. Smerdon studied our management at Thorn Farm. He looked over the cattle and agreed that they were in fine fettle. He showed great interest in the way in which the grass land was being managed. I had divided the fields into small paddocks by the use of electric fences. This method was not in general use on the edge of Dartmoor, although I had been using it for quite a long time on the farms on which I had learned my trade. The new challenge would be to manage the grassland so that the sheep would have some pastures which were kept all to themselves, but would also follow the dairy herd in order to scavenge the grass left by the more selective dairy cows. Mr. Smerdon was concerned that sheep might not honour the presence of electric fences in the same way that cows do. But after a warming cup of tea we shook hands on the deal. The handshake was, to the farming community, as binding as a sealed covenant. I was invited me to join him at Newton Abbot market the following week.

We met in the busy market place a week later. My mind slipped back to that day years before when I had ventured into the ancient market place of Battle. Working together, we selected our choice. Mr. Smerdon's great experience ensured that we bought the ewes at the right price. The art of bidding for livestock in the markets of England is one which is only learned from experience. Even the language of the auctioneer needs to be understood. "Sold to Mr. Smerdon," the auctioneer announced as he dropped his hammer sharply on the rostrum. With the purchase done I realised that I had become a shepherd.

The arrival of the sheep on the farm created great excitement for our dogs Nellie and Jug. They had become cow dogs rather than sheep dogs since we had left Perrotts Brook Farm. Now they would be fulfilled, I thought, because these Collie's are bred for the purpose of working with sheep. We soon discovered that whilst Thorn Farm was well fenced to retain cows in the pastures chosen for them, our cross-bred Dartmoor and Clun Forest ewes were adept at escaping. The moorland side of their character ensured that they were great escapologists. For them the grass on the other side of the hedge was always greener. Mr. Smerdon referred to them as 'woolly jumpers'. We referred to them as 'Smerdon's girls'.

Before long it was clear there was a tyrant among them, a despotic leader ewe who would always be at the centre of any movements to outwit us. She would exploit any weak spot in the hedgerow or reverse her woolly backside into the electric fencing wire, the shock of which her wool seemed to insulate her from. She would then push herself backwards until she had 'sheepdozed' an escape hole, or broken the electric fence. We named her Agatha. She caused us an awful lot of trouble, but one day Agatha went too far.

She had given birth to her first lamb which was barely a month old. She set out to teach it the skills that she had acquired. During the night, Agatha, evading the constant attention of the other members of the flock, engineered a daring escape. Her spirit of adventure caused her to invade the land owned by Mr. Brimblecombe, a neighbouring farmer.

I had counted the sheep at sundown, as was my custom. They had appeared to be contented and were all present. On my visit next morning, I was puzzled to find that two were missing. A further scrutiny confirmed that Agatha and her lamb had gone astray. I could find no trace of them. They were lost!

A search of the farm failed to locate the missing pair. Having sent Nell and Jug to search among the bramble, thorn and bracken in the rough land, I made my way to the top of Heltor rock, the landmark which straddled two farms. Far away I could hear a sheep and a lamb bleating. Although Mr. Brimblecombe's flock was grazing peacefully, the commotion was being caused by a single ewe with her lamb. They were obviously upset having been shut in a small pen near the farm house.

There was no doubt that Agatha and her lamb had been taken prisoner by Mr. Brimblecombe! It was, I surmised, only a matter of time before I received a phone call to ask me to remove my lost sheep and pay him compensation for their overnight gluttony at his expense.

Valerie and I decided that we would attempt to rescue Aggie and her lamb and, if possible, without being noticed by Mr. Brimblecombe. We could see no sign of him. As it was market day in Exeter we hoped that he might well be away from home. Feeling like commandoes, we covertly crawled and climbed our way across Brimblecombe's farm, keeping ourselves hidden behind the hedgerows. The distance was about a quarter of a mile. Watching all the time for any movement from our neighbours we slowly reached the pen where our property was held in a rustic prison.

Agatha greeted us enthusiastically. There was very little grass for her to eat in the place of her captivity. Valerie, who was always fast and athletic in action, chased and caught the lamb. I did a rugby tackle on Agatha and, although she was heavy, hoisted her onto my shoulders. We manhandled the two escapees across the many obstacles that lay between their prison and the remainder of Smerdon's girls.

Arriving back on Thorn Farm we received a hero's welcome. Looking across the fields and up to Aggie's prison later than day, we could see Mr. Brimblecombe standing with his hands on his hips, gazing across to where our sheep were once again grazing peacefully. They were all present and their escape route had been repaired. Although we met and worked together with our neighbour on many occasions in the days that followed, the capture and rescue of Agatha was never ever mentioned.

A few days later, whilst dipping once more into the fascinating contents of Valerie's New English Bible, I was to read the stories about the Good Shepherd and the parable of the lost sheep. We had rescued Agatha and in later years that rescue suddenly meant a very great deal to me.

Unwanted Changes

The fixed routine of farm life could never be changed. The arrival of relatives and friends was thus a welcome break. But all who came were expected to enter into the daily chores in the farm house and on the farm. Valerie's cousins, Mike Clarkson and Malcolm Gascoigne, each contributed a great amount of heavy labour. Mike's principle contribution was the clearing of many huge rocks from the meadows that were to be re-seeded. Using Nippit, the Standard Fordson tractor, and an old anchor chain, he cleared 'Pride and Joy' field of its worst obstacles. Malcolm Gascoigne also showed great promise as a farmer. We wondered if he would end up as a permanent partner in the business. Eventually he found his future supervising safaris in Kenya. Mike went on into the business of renovating houses and cottages.

My brother Edward enjoyed the farm too. Being smitten with jaundice and facing a deadline for his book 'The Battle of Britain', he abandoned London and escaped to the peace and quiet of the countryside in order to complete his task. This year's winter was long and cold. By the time the book was finished our entire stock of logs, on which we depended for warmth in the house, had been consumed. While this was a burden for the farm's economy, our reward was to see the book published on time and selling well.

On one occasion Ed was seated in the kitchen wearing only a dressing gown and, oddly, a tea cosy on his head in order to contain body heat! I brought Bob Carr, the much loved and respected Moretonhampstead vet, into the welcoming warmth of the kitchen for a reviving cup of tea. Observing my brother in such strange clothing, I introduced him as my grandmother. Bob took my introduction at face value and shaking hands with this strange looking person greeted 'her' with the words "I do hope that you are enjoying life on the farm, Mrs. Bishop." Ed's laugh, which resembled the sound that a hen makes when she has just laid an egg, resounded across the hills and valleys of Devonshire.

Ron and Ann Bundle, with their children Richard, Simon and Sarah, arrived on one occasion just as our four acre field of Scotch seed potatoes were ready for harvesting. Having a willing squad of workers to call upon I was able to remain aboard the Ferguson tractor, which had a mounted potato spinner attached. This was a luxury for me because the job was tedious and slow when our usual work force (Valerie and I) was on its own.

The Bundles bent their backs intent on picking the potatoes and tipping them into the hessian bags ready for transportation down to the barn. Later, when it became dark, we would have to sort and grade them by hand. I rode by in majesty giving them no respite. As soon as they had finished picking up a long row of earthy spuds, another row of freshly lifted ones was awaiting their attention. They were rewarded with fish and chips for the farm house tea that followed. The chips were from our own potatoes which we had sold to the owner of the fish and chip shop in Moretonhampstead.

These were happy times but clouds were gathering. Our established, productive and profitable dairy herd began failing the statutory test to affirm that they were free of the dreaded disease tuberculosis. One by one they failed to pass the Tuberculin test. All dairy cows that failed it again after a second test had to be slaughtered. A downward spiral of lost milk production and vital income followed.

The milk cheque was the mainstay of our cash flow. Each time there was a retest another of our much loved and best animals succumbed. The tension became very great. Bob Carr and Gordon Shattock, our veterinary advisors, were at a loss to explain this disastrous sequence of events. We learned that the disease was almost certainly contracted from the badgers that were established in ancient setts located amongst the rocks and bracken on the wild area of the farm. We fenced around the area and kept the herd away from it as much as possible. We ended up losing over a third of our most productive and much loved animals. In time the situation improved and the stress began to ease. We brought in replacement cows in order to boost our milk production and thus maintain our vital monthly milk cheques.

At the same time my knee, which had always been subject to pain and swelling after a hard day's work, inflamed more frequently. Eventually it became so sore that it was not possible for me to walk. Our doctor ordered complete rest. I was essentially disabled. I watched Valerie becoming tired and despondent as she bravely struggled to combine the jobs of mother and farmer.

A week or two before Easter, Dr. Glyn Jones, who had been a tower of strength to us, stood at the end of our bed holding on to my big toe. He looked at me kindly and said, "You know I think that you and Valerie have got to do some hard thinking." He told us that my knee was dangerously inflamed and that I must not do any more heavy manual work. Unless I could afford to pay a man to undertake the heavy work for me I should seriously consider giving up farming. The alternative was the possibility that I might lose my leg.

The farm was not yet financially strong enough for us to employ a full time assistant. Dr. Jones kindly, but firmly, counselled that we should accept the fact that we would have to abandon our beloved little kingdom. Thorn Farm had brought into being the fulfilment of our ambition to own a farm of our own. But it appeared that it was soon to be all over. The gloom and depression was overwhelming. The tears flowed and we could find no solace. What could I do? I was not trained for anything else and we could not imagine how our little family could find anything else that we wanted to do in the future.

As the hard and busy days of early spring progressed, Valerie's strength and health began to weaken. My right knee showed little sign of healing and the close of our farming adventure became more and more imminent. The daily chores of the dairy herd precluded participation in any peripheral activities.

We still faced monumental decisions. To whom could we now turn? My parents were gone. Valerie's parents had retired, but still ran a small pub, the Red Lion, in Shobrooke, near Crediton, in Devonshire. But we did not feel that we were the right sort of people to make a success of managing a Public House. The farm, our dairy herd, the sheep, working dogs and household pets were our life's work. To loose them would bring our farming dream to an end.

Valerie recalls that it was while we were still in bed and sleepy early on Easter morning that I turned to her and said "I don't know what I can do if we loose the farm. I'm not trained to do anything else. But if I can't farm I'd like to do something in which I can help other people. Perhaps I could train to be a Children's Officer, or …" Here I hesitated and then continued shyly "or even find out how I could serve within the Church in some capacity." She wondered if perhaps I was out of my mind! She knew how negative and critical I had always been of clergymen, but she made no comment.

Soon after Easter we took the sad decision to offer up Thorn Farm for sale. The reality of what we were about to do led to a new concern. Having borrowed practically all the capital with which to finance our farming business, could we expect to recoup sufficient funds to pay off our debts? We had reinvested our profits each year back into the business in order to increase milk production and improve the grassland so that we could buy more cows.

The tuberculin breakdown in the Ayrshire herd had been a disaster, but we reclaimed the situation and the herd was in full production again. The Thorn Farm Ayrshires had won the distinction of becoming the highest yielding herd on a small farm in the County of Devon.

The Property Agents to whom we turned for advice carried out a careful survey of our property. They presented us with the facts concerning our proposed sale. They informed us it would be an awesome gamble. The possibility was that by the time we had sold the farm, the dairy herd, the tractors and the equipment, we might end up fifteen hundred pounds in debt. A fair sale could cause us to break even. Then the good news came. If everything went very well, we might emerge from the venture with fifteen hundred pounds in hand. It was a difficult decision to take. We determined to take the risk. A 'For Sale' sign soon adorned the entrance to our farm lane.

Arrangements were made for an 'on farm' sale of our dairy herd and their calves. The pigs, chickens, everything, had to go. We were to haul all our farm tractors and equipment into the fields nearest the farm house in preparation for their sale by auction. The day of the sale was chosen and our many wonderful friends rallied round to come to our aid.

The farming community gave us tremendous support and encouragement. Like us they wondered what the future would hold as we prepared for the disposal of the farmhouse and land. The meadows were looking gloriously green and productive. Six years of hard work and dedication to farm improvement had transformed a derelict Devonshire farm into a respected and well farmed marginal hill farm.

There was still a great deal to be done. But now someone else would come forward to take up the challenge. The farm routine, which had been sustained so faithfully over the six years that had passed, was now undertaken with a feeling of sadness and despair as we waited for the day of the sale.

The day of the sale dawned. The weather was dreary. A Dartmoor mist shrouded the farm. Heltor Rock was not even visible from our bedroom window, a fact which usually forecast a rainy day. Would anyone come to the sale? The thought of a bad sale and a deficit of over a thousand pounds were unbearable.

Milking the cows for the last time brought us a tremendous sense of impending bereavement. By evening they would all be in new surroundings, being milked by strangers, and far away from the farm where many of them had been born and bred. The milking having been accomplished, the cow family was turned out to graze for the last time. But only for a while for there soon would be a change in their routine.

After breakfast they were surprised to be rounded up and returned to the farmyard. Our best friends, Geoff Baines and Peter Morris, arrived and insisted that they had come to help get the cows ready for the sale. They set to work giving each animal's tail a splendid haircut with a fluffy tassel that made them look very handsome. Then they gave each, by now inquiring, member of the herd a shampoo. They were washed and scrubbed from head to tail. Soon they were holding their heads high, as if aware how beautiful they looked. Little did they know that they would soon face the appraising eyes of those who would become their new owners!

A motley collection of farm implements and tools were laid out in rows in the meadow and, apart from the Ferguson tractor which had also been washed and polished, most of it looked like a load of junk. Still the weather glowered over the farm and the famous Dartmoor mist looked as if it was set in for the day. As the time of the sale drew near I walked up to the field at the top of the lane, which had been sign-posted as the parking area for the sale. It was empty. Would anyone come? I sensed disaster and began to tremble with a foreboding that we were about to be in deep trouble. Geoff and Pete did their best to encourage us and tried to cheer us up over a warming cup of coffee.

Next the auctioneer and his assistants arrived. They admired the clean and shining herd of Ayrshire cows, each member of which watched every movement around them. Somehow the family of cows concealed their own anxiety by placidly chewing their cud. They were plainly aware that this day was different, but although cows are always full of curiosity it was obvious they had no idea concerning the dramatic changes that were about to take place in their bovine lives.

The auctioneer looked at his watch. Geoff, who had taken a walk to the car park, returned with a grin on his face. "They're arriving," he said cheerfully.

"Are there many?" I asked him anxiously.

"Yes," he replied. "They're pouring in."

As he spoke the first of many of our friends from neighbouring farms could be seen casting a professional eye over all that we had prepared for the sale. There were also those who had come from afar looking for some good replacements for their own herds.

The auctioneer rang his bell to mark the fact that the sale would begin in five minutes time. Everyone took up strategic places alongside the professionally prepared sale ring in anticipation. Suddenly the sun broke through the mist and bathed the farm in a radiant and golden light. I recall a moment of wonder, and even joy, as the warmth of a beautiful day and a special glowing light fell on the assembled dairy cows. They looked just beautiful as they basked in a natural spotlight made of sunbeams.

The sale began. One by one the cows and calves were led into the ring where, adorned in a new long cotton white coat, I presented them to their prospective buyers. The bidding was brisk and keen. Within minutes I sensed that we were going to be successful in paying off all our debts. At about the half way stage of the sale the auctioneer whispered to me "That's covered all your liabilities. Everything that's sold now is your profit." Our farm sale had been successful. We were full of gratitude and appreciation towards our friends and neighbours who had worked hard to make this happen.

The vital sum of about £1,500 together with the sale of the farm ensured that we would be able to payoff the mortgage with funds to spare. When we left our beloved Thorn Farm at least we would leave with some extra capital which would provide us a financial cushion. The sale ended and the crowds drifted away. The cattle trucks that had been waiting expectantly to transport the animals to their new homes arrived and loaded their disturbed passengers.

That evening the silence of an empty farm was difficult to bear. The silence felt eerie and hauntingly unfamiliar. There was no work to do. Everything was over except for the cleaning up, which our fine neighbours were hard at work completing. Our six happy but stressful years as owners of a small patchwork of Devonshire countryside were over. Now we faced a new challenge as we wondered what the future would bring.

Refugees at Newcross

Thorn Farm was purchased by another young man intent on making his climb up the farming ladder. The fact that he did not appear to have much experience in farm management worried me. We had invested so many gruelling hours of hard work on that little patch of England that we had become covetous of it. We came to terms with the fact that it was now part of our history and there was no point in looking back. We wished him good fortune.

The farm was sold with vacant possession so we had to move out as soon as possible. Our immediate need was to find housing. We didn't know where to start. In addition to the housing issue, we didn't have any idea as to what our future would hold. Collectively, these problems were eased and address by a group of individuals: John and Marjorie Hebditch at Newcross, Sir John and Lady Langman at Perrotts Brook, and Miss Catherine Daniel in Maperton, Somerset.

The Hebditchs suggested that we should rent a small caravan. They offered us a site on their farm at Newcross, not too far from the farm house. There we could set up our temporary home as refugees. John had discovered that we could rent a caravan from a local dealer. The rent would cost us £5 a week. He chose a sheltered corner in a nearby field where we could establish our new Romany home.

Being back at Newcross again after so many years was a strange feeling. The caravan was twenty feet in length and was equipped with a Calor Gas cooker. The beds doubled up as sofas during the day time. There was a separate little cubicle at one end which Timothy claimed as his. He had his own window and, unlike us, he was very excited at the prospect of living in so small a home amongst the cows and sheep. The toilet was in a little outside wooden hut, to which I had often gone in the past. It had been a place of quiet and reflection in those far off days and out of necessity it had become so again. It was imperative that I found a job as soon as possible. The small amount of capital that we had been fortunate to receive from the farm sale would certainly ebb away as the weeks passed.

A former neighbour at Thorn Farm, Robin Malim, had become involved in a farmers group trading company. He offered me a job driving an oil delivery truck which was about to begin delivering Gulf Oil supplies to farms at low cost. This was a tempting offer but we decided that it would not enable me to get out and try to solve the ultimate problem concerning our future. What could an injured farmer do if he couldn't farm? My formal education was almost non-existent. I had been at work on farms since the age of fifteen. Farming was the only job and way of life that I knew. Robin's enterprise began without me. His business became Valcourt Farms, a prosperous organisation based on the concept of the power of bulk buying.

There were several pointers as to my possible future. I had been working in a voluntary capacity for the Milk Marketing Board. This was the organisation which, at that time, bought and sold all the milk produced on Britain's farms. National milk sales had been dropping and I had been recruited to help promote sales. This was to be done by visiting women's clubs and schools and giving a talk about dairy farming and milk production. I had enjoyed doing these and had been successful in that there had been a good response for my effort. My experience of taking part in Young Farmers Club public speaking competitions, an activity in which John Hebditch had encouraged me, had developed my self confidence. The once very shy young man could now stand up and address an audience, although it always was, and has remained, an activity which I find to be stressful.

The National Farmers Union was advertising for applicants who would be interested in becoming Group Secretaries. The work would be that of supporting local farmers, together with arranging insurance for their farming enterprises. A reasonably good salary would be paid and augmented by commission on the insurance policies sold. I applied for one of these jobs, but on reflecting on the role that I would be required to play, I felt that it was not for me. The Farmers Union felt the same way! My application was not successful.

One morning John came across to the caravan carrying a copy of 'The Farmer's Weekly'. Excitedly he showed me an advertisement which stated that the Milk Marketing Board was looking for Milk Promotion Officers. The task assigned would be to encourage milk sales for the Board on a regional basis. This seemed to be a very real lead. This was an activity in which I had already been involved.

I was also following up opportunities in work beyond the farming world. I set out to discover how I might pursue a training programme that would equip me to undertake some kind of social work. Could I become a Children's Officer or even join the Probation Service? As I pursued these possibilities my hopes faded. I came to a dead end. I did not have the required educational qualifications in order to qualify for entry to a training college.

Suppressed beneath all these other ideas was something that I found hard to identify or express. There was something deep and mysterious within me, trying to guide me. I could not understand the innermost yearning that was disturbing me except that it was relevant to all the thoughts that I had pondered since becoming engrossed in the writings in the Bible's New Testament. I was still regularly continuing my reading of Valerie's birthday present from years before, the New English Bible. The stories and parables of Jesus of Nazareth, the events recorded in The Acts of the Apostles, and the writings of Saint Paul and the other letter writers, although beyond my comprehension, pointed to a different way of life. I can not claim to have been able to elucidate what was going on within my mind and my heart. I clearly didn't know.

John Hebditch was a devoted member of his Congregational Church at East Lambrook. He and Marjorie had often invited me to join them on Sunday mornings when I worked on their farm. I had declined to do so although I did venture once or twice to the local Church of England services. I remember thinking, incorrectly I'm sure, that the family's Sunday morning at Chapel was a time when they needed to be together. On Sunday mornings I could have an hour to myself. I would enjoy spending time alone in their pleasant home and, while no one was there, play the piano all alone, picking my way through the popular tunes of the time.

We could hear the church bells ringing from the nearby villages from our caravan home and I noticed that the Hebditchs would still faithfully make their way to the Chapel. One Sunday morning, Valerie and I asked if we could go with them.

The country people who assembled in this interesting chapel were continuing a tradition and ritual that had been practiced for generations. As we shared in their worship I listened to the bible readings. They sang the old hymns and the Minister said his extempore prayers. There was a transcendence and glory in the practical and down to earth form of worship as they lifted their hearts to Almighty God. I was moved by their fervour and humility. At last I was in touch with that 'something' that was causing me so much inner disturbance.

After chapel we were invited to an excellent Sunday lunch, a meal that had been such a feature of past days when the whole family gathered. After the farm house lunch I consulted John, for whom I had a deep respect and affection. As I attempted to describe my personal dilemma concerning the future, I felt inadequate at putting my feelings into words. John appeared to understand and suggested that I might be able to get some help from Catherine Daniel, who had been so kind to me in the past. He explained that he knew that she was a leading person in the local Church of England circles. "Perhaps she could help you" he kindly suggested.

Catherine Daniel, a farmer, had been supportive to me when I was a teenager on the farm at North Cheriton in Somerset. She had been one of the members of the congregation at the Reverend Tom Langley's village church. Tom Langley had been the village parson who had braved the gale, the rain and the mud to visit me on that day years before, as I loaded Mangold roots, and to whom I had confided that I felt that one day I would like to do the same kind of work that he was doing.

Tom had reacted strongly at the time, saying that I should put such ideas out of my head because I would never be considered eligible given my lack of education. Now Tom himself was out of reach. He and his wife Monica, who had been such a strength and comfort to me during one of the loneliest periods of my young life, had returned to work in South Africa. He was now the Archdeacon of Pretoria.

Miss Daniel was surprised to hear from me for we had not been in touch for years. "Why don't you and Valerie come over and have supper with me?" she invited. I accepted gratefully. Our visit was arranged for a few days later.

North Cheriton had not changed during the passing of the years. Valerie and I arrived early and made our way to the parish church of Saint Peter and Saint Paul in Maperton. This church is now a member of a group of churches known as the Camelot parishes in the diocese of Bath and Wells. As we entered we experienced a feeling of quiet and peace. I had attended church there once and recalled being strangely moved by the sincerity with which Tom Langley had taken the service. That he took a great deal of trouble to present a beautiful and dignified liturgy, despite the fact that there were only a handful of people in church, seemed rather wonderful.

As we stood in the aisle looking down the chancel towards the sanctuary, I felt a deep emotional stirring within the depths of my being. This feeling was beyond my understanding but it was as though I was in communication with a new presence in my life.

Miss Daniel welcomed us in her matter of fact and charming way. After an excellent meal we lingered over coffee. We related our experiences on Thorn Farm and our present troubles. Valerie knew that I wanted to broach the difficult question concerning my future. Lingering shyness and timidity stood as a barrier between what I was saying and what I needed to say.

Valerie later admitted that if she had been able to kick me under the table she would have done so. The time passed swiftly and it was towards midnight. Still I had not asked the question that was waiting to escape into the freedom of reality. Eventually I could hold back no longer.

"I really want to ask you something very important to me," I said, "but I don't know how to say it."

"Oh Michael," Miss Daniel responded, "That sounds interesting." She paused attentively as if giving me the encouragement and the moment in which to reveal my burning question.

My back was to the wall. As my heart thudded against my chest I stammered out the question. "What do I have to do if I want to work full time for the church?"

"What do you mean?" she asked gently. "Do you want to become a priest?"

I had never uttered the word even to myself and didn't really understand what being a priest implied. "I don't think that's what I want to do" I said. I tried to describe the disturbance that had been within me for so many months since that Easter morning when we had decided that we must sell the farm.

"Michael" she said, "That's not a job. It's what we call a vocation. It's as if God might be calling you into a special role." She paused. "Does it feel like that to you?"

She had illuminated the feeling that I had within me. "Yes" I replied. "It does feel a bit like that."

She took my hand and said quietly "The Bishop of Bath and Wells is a good friend of mine. I'll have a talk with him in the morning and ask his advice. He may, perhaps, want to meet with you."

As we made our way home to the caravan a new day was dawning. We kept a mutual tryst of silence between us. Unbeknown to us our future was being created.

A Choice of Ladders

While it took some time for it to dawn upon my mind, I was clearly confronted by a choice of new ladders. I had climbed the farming ladder to its highest rung. The ladders now before me contained an unknown number of rungs because the tops of them were shrouded in a mist of mystery. What would our future be? Would my lack of formal education bring about the breaking of a rung?

The Bishop of Bath and Wells, known affectionately by the people in his Diocese as 'Jock' Henderson, received a telephone call from Miss Daniel the following morning. Later in the day she telephoned me to say that the Bishop's engagements at the moment made it impossible for him to meet with me. But he had asked Prebendary Kingsnorth, his Director of Candidates for Ordination, to contact me to arrange a meeting in order that he could advise me.

My thoughts were transported back to the many times in which I had evaded the Vicar of Bridford. I actually felt terror at the sighting of anyone wearing one of those forbidding round, back to front collars, known by the public as 'dog collars', which are worn by the clergy of the Church of England.

Prebendary Kingsnorth was the epitome of all my fears. His black suit, the collar and his visage struck utter terror into my soul. Fortunately, Father Kingsnorth's outward appearance was softened by the kindliness in his eyes and the gentleness of his voice. He wanted to hear my story and he listened to it patiently.

Pensively he began to respond to it. "Well Michael, that's very interesting. It certainly seems as if your reading of the Bible has evoked a wonderful response. But do you ever go to church?" I had to admit that I didn't attend church. He sat with his hands clasped, as though in prayer. "I am also concerned by your lack of education" he commented. My heart thumped hard and an echo of the remark made by Tom Langley, the parish priest at Maperton, sounded in my brain.

A cup of tea in his hand and a time of social chatter which included Valerie followed. Father Kingsnorth, to whom I had warmed, turned his attention to Valerie. "How do your feel about all this?" he asked her.

The woman who had married a farmer, who loved the farm life and the countryside, replied "If it's what is right for Michael and it's what he wants to do, I shall be at his side to support him."

Making ready to go on his way, Father Kingsnorth took my hand in farewell. "I've enjoyed meeting you both," he said. "I will be putting your name forward as a candidate to attend the next CACTM Selection conference, Michael." He explained that the CACTM was the Church's Advisory Committee for the Ministry, which is the Board whose task it is to select candidates for training into the priesthood. "I can't say what their decision might be" he concluded, "but I must impress upon you that I think that it will be very unlikely that you will be selected. But that's not for me to decide. I'll send you details of the Selection Conference as soon as possible."

My foot was on the bottom rung of one of the ladders. Meanwhile my inquiries regarding a job in the public relations department of the Milk Marketing Board had borne fruit. Having received my Curriculum Vitae, the Board had invited me to an interview at their headquarters in Thames Ditton. CACTM had also invited me to attend a three day Selection Conference. I was to attend at the Southwark Diocesan Retreat House in Bletchingley on the afternoon of the first day. The interview with the Milk Marketing Board was to begin on the morning of that same day. My destiny might be decided within a very short time.

The day on which I must face both selection conferences dawned. Taking leave of Valerie and young Tim in our caravan home, I climbed into our MG Magnet car. Feeling tremendously alone, I set off for the Milk Board's Headquarters. As I drove through the great gates which adorned the grounds of the Milk Board's empire, I was intrigued by the excellence and luxury of the Head Office and its grounds. My thoughts went out to all Britain's dairy farmers, in their sometimes rather dilapidated farm houses, whose hard work and farming skills had been the source of all this magnificence.

On arrival I discovered that I was in competition with three other applicants. They each seemed to be very charming and I began to doubt my chance of success. A secretary showed us into a small office and said that we would be interviewed in alphabetical order. B for Bishop ensured that I would be the first in. The secretary led me along a corridor and into the boardroom.

Sir Richard Trehearne, the President, sat in an impressive chair behind a highly polished conference table. He was flanked on each side by two Directors. My shyness nearly overwhelmed me and my knees wobbled as I felt the intense scrutiny to which I was being subjected. The secretary nodded towards a comfortable looking leather chair placed directly in front of the great man whose name I had seen so often on the cheques received in payment for the hundreds of gallons of milk I had sold to the Board.

The President noted my farming past and I was subjected to a discreet inquiry as to whether my farm had been successful. I offered to show the farm accounts and I flourished the Marketing Board's own handbook which showed my Thorn Farm Ayrshire herd as having been the most productive herd for its size in Devonshire.

The details of the position that was being offered were read out to me by another Director. The financial package offered was presented by the Board's Secretary. The work and the salary offered was music to the ears of a former self-employed dairy farmer. £18,000 a year, a company car and assistance with the down payment on a home would be offered. Our farm profits had never realised anything approaching this salary. In addition, I would have a normal working week and free weekends. If I was successful all my problems would be solved and next week we would be visiting agents in search of our new house.

The interview was over in a surprisingly short time and I felt that I had fielded the questions well and even managed to amuse the interviewers. I was asked to return to the office and send in the next candidate. The time passed slowly as one by one my fellow competitors went into their own interviews. When all four interviews had been completed the secretary assured us that the Board would be making the appointment as soon as possible. All we could do was wait and chat together nervously, generously wishing one another good fortune.

The secretary reappeared and we all held our breath. Who was it to be? "Mr. Bishop, would you care to return to the boardroom?" Turning to the others she said "Any you can all leave except for Mr. Davidson, our second choice, who I am instructed to request to stay for a few minutes just in case there are any problems or last minute hitches with regards to Mr. Bishop's appointment."

The other hopeful applicants generously shook my hand and wished me luck. Mr. Davidson took his seat again certain that his application had failed. Surely it was just a matter of time before he would be on his way home too.

In the boardroom Sir Richard Trehearne stood up and came to greet me. Shaking my hand vigorously, he said cheerfully "Well done Bishop, well done. We'll be seeing you again! Now we'll leave Mr. Wainwright to go through the details with you and begin the business of setting you up as our new representative in Trowbridge, Somerset. You'll need to find yourself a nice house. It's a lovely area!"

A whispered conversation between Mr. Wainwright and Sir Richard ensued. Mr. Trehearne turned back to me. "I quite forgot" he said. "I assume you are accepting our offer."

My mind was in turmoil. My Selection Conference for the Church was due to begin later in the day. What should I do? "I wonder Sir," I pleaded "If I could postpone making a decision for a few days?"

The President's mouth dropped open in surprise. "Why?" he asked. "Do you have a better offer elsewhere?"

"No Sir," I replied, "But I must be honest and tell you that this evening I begin another selection conference. I am attending a three day assessment to decide if I am a suitable person to enter training for entry into full time ministry for the Church of England."

Mr. Trehearne's surprised look changed to one of dismay. Hurriedly he gathered his fellow Directors around him. They conferred in whispers. Turning back to me and calling me by my first name for the first time, the man who had almost become my new boss replied, "Michael, I can see the dilemma that you are in, but I'm very sorry you will have to give us a definite answer now. We have the runner up waiting and if you decline we will have to offer the job to him."

My mind centred on Valerie and Tim waiting anxiously in our makeshift caravan home. I thought of the standard of living and financial security that this great new opportunity would bring to them, but something held me back from accepting. I don't know how long I delayed my answer but when it came it felt as if my words were coming from beyond myself. It was almost as if a voice from deep within me was speaking. "Well Sir," I heard the voice saying, "In that case I must decline your offer. I cannot accept until I have had my vocation to serve in the Church denied or accepted."

"Then I'm very sorry" said Trehearne. "You are by far the best candidate. Would you care to go and tell Mr. Davidson to come along? I'll have to offer him the position now that you have declined it."

"Yes," I replied. "But if I am rejected by the Church can I reapply for a similar post?"

"Yes you can," he answered. "But I must warn you these appointments are very few and far between and you may not be the best candidate on the next occasion." I thanked him, wondering what utter foolishness had made me decline the chance of a lifetime. Mr. Davidson made his way to the boardroom to accept the post that I had rejected. I have often wondered how he prospered!

I returned to my car and sat quietly for a while. I was exhausted and depressed. I wondered how I would break the news to Valerie. I had turned down the very job that I needed and had very little prospect of being accepted for training by the Church. Looking at my map, I planned my journey to Bletchingley.

Once there I was greeted at the door by a man wearing a long black cassock. Canon Rhymes, Warden of the Southward Diocesan Retreat House showed me to a small and sparse, but pleasant, bedroom. "There's a cup of tea in the Common Room," he told me. "Our first session is at five o'clock."

The Common Room was already occupied by a motley group of men of all ages and sizes wearing a variety of kinds of clothing. There were about twenty of us. Some wore jeans and brightly coloured shirts. Others, in contrast, wore business suits and striped shirts. The words spoken between us demonstrated that my fellow applicants were from all walks of life and represented a wide spectrum of the regions of the British Isles.

Each newcomer was warmly welcomed by those who had already settled in. Friendly grins, firm handshakes and small talk filled the hour that elapsed before an elderly man wearing the traditional Church of England 'dog collar' entered. I noticed that he was wearing a rather nice shirt that was purple. I was about to meet a Bishop of the Church of England for the first time.

As we settled into our chairs, which were placed in a semicircle, we could see that there were five selectors present. They were all men and, as they introduced themselves, we learned that in addition to the Bishop we were confronted by a parish priest, a Director of a well known company, a churchwarden of a parish church, and another man who we later learned was a doctor, possibly, we thought, a psychologist.

Next it was our turn. We were asked to introduce ourselves. We were each to have a period of two minutes in order to say who we were and give a summary of our life experience. We discovered that amongst those present we had a famous actor, an undertaker, a librarian, several business men, a dentist, an architect and a taxi driver. I was the only countryman and immediately received the title of 'The Farmer'. My introduction included full disclosure about my brief schooling, which caused a lengthy silence. As with the interview earlier in the day, I was embarrassed to see that every eye was focused on me. I imagined that the selectors looked a little puzzled and whilst they had been making notes when the others had been speaking, their pencils were not used during my presentation.

The session ended and a school like meal was served after which we all attended the late evening service of Compline. Following the service, which I found to be an emotional experience, I retired to my room for an anxious and disturbed night, but I found comfort by the prayer 'Guide us waking, O Lord, and guard us sleeping.'

The days passed as each of the selectors worked through their interviews with the postulants. I was a little concerned to be termed a postulant. This was a word

I had not heard before and I didn't know its meaning. My last interview was with the Bishop. Arriving at the door of his room at the appointed time, I timidly gave it a gentle knock only to receive no response. I knocked louder. Again there was no response. Another postulant passed by. Seeing me waiting at the door, he said gently "Just go in."

Timidly I opened the door and peered in. The Bishop was on his knees by the open window. His eyes were closed and he did not move. I gave a quiet cough which elicited no response. I thought that he might be asleep. Being unable to decide what to do, I crossed the room and stood there for a few moments. There being no response I nearly retreated, but something made me kneel down. After a few moments the Bishop stirred. "How's your prayer life my boy?" he asked.

I had never been conscious of saying anything except the formal prayers that I had said with others on my infrequent visits to church. "Not very good Bishop," I replied. I was certain at that moment that I should have accepted the post with the Milk Marketing Board.

When the selection conference was over, I made my way home to Newcross. I had only my rejection of the Milk Board's offer to report to Valerie. The Bishop had said I would hear the decision of the Selection Board in about ten days time. All we could do was to wait.

The Challenge

Ten days had passed and still there was no sign of a letter or a telephone call from the Church's Advisory Committee. Uncertainty about the future is a difficult emotion to handle. I was burdened by the thought that I had made a dreadful mistake in declining the job with the Milk Marketing Board. We decided to go down to the Old Coach House in Shobrooke, where Jack and Audrey Spurway now lived, to spend a few days away from our little home in a field.

On arrival we received a warm welcome which was always a certainty there. The family dogs would bark joyously and race round in circles. Dad Spurway was always prepared with some surprise for Tim whose great grin would be at its best.

The cosy home smelt strongly of tobacco smoke and there, sure enough, was Dad's pipe, from which he never parted, sticking out of the corner of his mouth. "Oh by the way Mike," Audrey remarked as we entered the small front hall, "There's a letter for you on the table. It's been here for a few days."

Could it be the one that we were awaiting? My hands shook as I opened the official looking envelope. 'We are glad to inform you that you have been accepted as a candidate for training.' As I read on, the first moment of elation subsided. Acceptance was provisional. I would have to prove my vocation. I should link up, I was instructed, with an approved parish church and put myself under the direction of the Rector. I should also prove my academic capability by passing at least two General Certificate of Education examinations at the Ordinary Level. The subjects should be English and Religious knowledge.

My immediate reaction was one of deep despair. Here, right at the beginning, the weakness of my position was highlighted. I did not have any association with a church, and I had as yet no educational attainments. My folly in declining the excellent prospects offered by the Milk Marketing Board appalled me more and more. Should I just drop the whole crazy adventure now? If I were continue in my quest where should I begin?

Valerie did her best to encourage and reassure me. She insisted that she had faith in me. She knew that I could do it. But what, I wondered, was IT? To whom could I turn for advice? I had a wife and family to support. The capital obtained from the farm sale was already being eaten away. How could I study and earn a living?

It was at this point that wonderful things began to happen A letter arrived from Sir John and Lady Langman. They would be going to Canada for a month. If we were still unemployed, would we consider moving into the guest room at Perrotts Brook House and act as caretakers while they were away? We were invited to go and spend the weekend with them in order to talk things over.

Valerie and I felt good being back at Perrotts Brook and seeing the farm. We discussed our future with John and Pamela over a delicious breakfast. It was agreed that we should take up residence for a month. In return for caretaking, we would have a delightful room and all our meals would be provided. The housekeeper would make sure that we had everything that we needed.

That evening, after dinner, Sir John said that he had some good news to share with us. "I've been in touch with Arthur Naylor. He's the Director of the YMCA Community Services. I've told him about you and he's quite interested. He runs a large hostel at the Royal Aircraft Establishment in Farnborough and he has a vacancy for an assistant warden."

Sir John went on to explain that the YMCA managed the hostel as the residential home for the young engineers, aged between sixteen and twenty years of age who where serving their apprenticeship at the Establishment. "You'll need a job Michael," he counselled. "And it will have to be one which will let you study for your exams, and also prove yourself in an occupation other than farming. If it works out you could link up with one of the local churches. I think that you should have a shot at it" he concluded.

The R.A.E. Apprentices Hostel in Farnborough was located on the fringe of the famous airfield where the latest civil and military aircraft were developed and tested. The young men, who were selected from amongst the most talented scholars from all over the United Kingdom, were housed in a former Royal Air Force barracks.

Arthur Naylor welcomed us to the Apprentices Hostel and introduced us to Mr. Roberts, the Warden. The vacant post was for an Assistant Warden. The Warden needed an assistant who would develop personal relationships with the residents. Being an intelligent and volatile group of young men they were frequently in need of pastoral care and friendship. There were also disciplinary problems to be tackled. The apprentices were subject to all kinds of troubles and emergencies.

This was a new post and I would have to learn how to do it as I went along! It was understood that I would be given time to study for my exams and that I would be linking myself with one of the local churches. Then the good news came. The salary was far more generous than I dared to hope and a small rent free bungalow was available on campus. Valerie and I had no doubts that if Mr. Naylor and Mr. Roberts would appoint me that we would take up the challenge.

A few days later our rented caravan home was towed away from Newcross Farm. Our MG Magnet car was loaded with our luggage and we said goodbye to John and Marjorie Hebditch.

The appointment would not commence for a few weeks and so we made our way to Perrotts Brook and spent the interval there enjoying the luxury and hospitality of the Langman's comfortable home. The time soon came for us to move on once more and make our way to Farnborough, in the County of Hampshire. The bungalow was pleasantly furnished. Tim had a real bedroom again and we were soon established in our new home.

Mr. Roberts introduced us to the residents at lunch time the next day. The young men were disturbingly quiet and were, we felt, hostile. The atmosphere was threatening and unfriendly and very soon it became obvious that I had taken on more of a challenge that I had realised.

That evening a group of apprentices appeared at the door of my office. They were complaining about the food. The toilets were not sanitary. "What," they demanded "are you going to do about it?"

I pleaded with them to give me time but promised to do my best for them. Next morning, the cleaners responsible for the bed-study rooms complained that engine parts were leaking oil on to the carpets and even the bed clothes. At the staff meeting with the Warden I was instructed to carry out surprise visits (he called them 'raids') on the boys bedrooms after dark. YMCA rules prohibited the boys from inviting girls onto the campus and it was my responsibility to apprehend any offenders. The police were frequently on the telephone passing on complaints about bad behaviour in the pubs and streets of the town. It seemed that everything that happened was blamed on the R.A.E. boys who were now my responsibility.

In these opening weeks many of the cleaning ladies resigned, including the supervisor. I was able to enlist Valerie's help. She became the new supervisor of the 'Mrs. Mops' and began a reign of friendly, yet strict, discipline along the corridors. I persuaded the R.A.E. to allow us the use of the empty workshops adjacent to the hostel, and in time most of the offending engine parts were allotted space there so that the greasy wardrobes could gradually be cleaned up. Workshops developed in which the spare time motor enthusiasts could build cars, repair motorbikes and invent all manner of devices.

Tim, now five years of age, became our ambassador and achieved our first breakthrough leading to friendlier relationships with our charges. Despite my attempts to improve the meals, they remained badly cooked and served. One day, as we were chewing our way through a tough slice of roast beef, I decided that the time had come for a showdown with the chef. Taking Tim with his plate of beef and armed with my own plate, I returned our lunch to the serving counter. The chef stood menacingly behind the counter. Every eye in the dining hall was on us. An angry chef brandished his carving knife menacingly at Tim, who then ran away, chased by the chef. After being rescued, Tim and I returned to the dining room. As we entered the assembled residents stood and clapped. The ice was broken. Tim celebrated the event by aiming his new toy racing car down the aisle between the dining tables and sending it hurtling towards the watching and appreciative audience. The car came to a halt. One young man stood up, bent down to the toy car, and sent it hurtling back across the room to Tim. The jeers which had at times greeted us in the dining room were replaced by a resounding cheer. The young man turned to his companions and then back towards us, and made a deep bow. Peace had been declared.

A new chef was needed and appointed. Although no one ever claimed that the food was great, the quality of the meals had improved and from that time on I received few complaints. Valerie's efficient leadership of the cleaning staff also led to great improvements in the bedrooms and toilets. The hostel had returned to a reasonably friendly and cooperative place.

One morning, three months later, Mr. Naylor arrived at the hostel with previous warning. Calling me into the Warden's office, he informed me that Mr. Roberts had left the hostel at very short notice. "You've established yourself as a very capable Assistant Warden, Michael," he told me. He continued by asking an unexpected question. "Do you think that you could manage to take over as Acting Warden for the next few months?"

I was now in charge of the hostel. Despite the many practical problems of administering the hostel, and the ever present personal problems which were now freely shared with me by many of the apprentices, I was able to establish a routine which allowed me to develop my own schedule of studies. I would spend the evenings in one of the small studies which the hostel provided for the apprentices to do my own studies in English and Religion. These GCE level studies were being guided under the caring and watchful eye of Wolsey Hall, a correspondence college based in Oxford.

Encouragement came with the return of my essays which began to be marked with remarks like 'Very good, keep it up' and even 'Excellent'. English grammar created more problems but in time I began to be awarded satisfactory marks for grammar too. The students assisted me on many occasions and were very supportive when they discovered that I was working to achieve my ambition of training to become a priest.

Religious studies proved more difficult. The course assumed that the student had acquired basic knowledge in Sunday Schools or at the Primary level. My memories of Old Ted's sermons at Langley Place and the religious education that I had received there were scant. But in time my marks improved.

I was unaware that day by day I was fulfilling the requirements of the Church Advisory Committee. I was enjoying my job and beginning to wonder whether I was being given an escape route. Could I not give service to God just as well from within the ranks of the YMCA? Ben Hutchinson, Rector of the Old Parish Church in Farnborough, and his wife Betty had other ideas for me.

The Old Parish Church

The apprentices' notice board contained a messy accumulation of faded cards. Among the telephone numbers for taxis and lost and found messages long since delivered, one faded card said simply 'Churches'. Two parish churches were listed. The one which appealed to me most simply read 'The Old Parish Church, Farnborough'. The phone number was Farnborough 600.

Back in my office my fingers hovered nervously over the telephone dial. I was about to face the moment that I dreaded most. I had not yet faced up to actual participation in the life, worship and work of a parish church. My fear of clergymen (clergyphobia?) was still as strong as ever. I knew that I would have to make the call so I dialled the number.

"Ben Hutchinson" announced a friendly and relaxed voice. "Can I help you?"

I remained silent for what seemed to be an age and then began hesitantly. "I need your advice. I have to link up with a local church. I have been accepted as an ordinand but have to achieve certain tasks before I can apply for training."

"Then we'd better meet. Are you in Farnborough?" he inquired. The Rector of the Old Parish Church said that he would be glad to meet me. I was invited to bring Valerie along too, for a chat.

We were greeted at the door of the Rectory by the warmest of welcomes. We could tell immediately that Ben and Betty Hutchinson were very special people. Our story was soon told. We felt at home and agreed that we would begin our life as brand new members of the congregation the following Sunday morning. "Come early though," counselled Betty, "because you may not get a seat otherwise!"

The sound of the chiming of the bells of the Old Parish Church will remain in my memory for ever. The sonorous 'five minute' bell seemed to vibrate into the depths of my soul. 'Come! Come! Come!' it seemed to call to me. Having entered the church we climbed over some rather ancient knees before we took our places situated behind a large stone pillar. The Bell ceased its persistent calling.

An excited silence fell upon the packed church. Then the majestic sound of the organ playing the opening bars of the hymn 'Praise my Soul the King of Heaven' was followed by the exciting sound of several hundred voices praising

God as if they really meant the words of praise that they were singing. My invitation had begun.

During the days ahead I was invited to attend the meetings of the various church groups. There were groups for prayer, groups for bible study and special training groups for those in varying stages of their development as members of this vibrant church. I was also invited to join the Rector's support team.

Ben Hutchinson had welcomed us with such warmth and enthusiasm that my 'clergyphobia' began to recede. I realised the immense strength and comfort that can be generated by a team of Christians learning and ministering under the guidance of a fine teacher. The final part of my unexpected pilgrimage into the church had commenced.

Before long I was surprised to find myself joining with those who came together regularly for a time spent in prayer. At first I was tense, self-conscious and, worse still, aware that my anxiety was being transmitted to my digestive system. The most embarrassing sounds of squeaks and rumbles, which to me echoed as if being amplified, disturbed my ability to experience the peace which the others present appeared to be sharing. Only my terror and shyness prevented me from bolting from the room.

My discomfort was heightened by another painful experience. One evening when the group had spent some minutes in an extended period of silent prayer, the door into our sanctuary of peace and quietness opened violently. Opening my eyes I saw that a young man was standing in the doorway with an expression of amazement on his face. He had one of the special haircuts of those times and his hair was bright green. As I looked around I noticed that several of my praying companions had assumed dramatic attitudes of prayer. Their arms were lifted in adoration: their faces were serene and smiling. I had never been brave enough to observe this before. I was intrigued by the scene around me. The young man was transfixed. He turned to some of his teenage companions who were standing behind him. "Cor!" he explained. "Come and look at this bunch of nutters!" As he slammed the door shut I detected no reaction from those who were praying beside me. At the close of the session they denied having noticed any interruption.

I was compelled to attempt to comprehend this experience. Was I amongst unbalanced people? This was a side of life I had never encountered before. My new friends were very ardent in prayer, but as soon as their prayers were over they became animated, joyful and appeared to be the happiest people that I had ever met. Being unable to come to any clear conclusion concerning the answer I put the question aside.

I could not help observing that the people with whom I now prayed, and from whom I was learning more and more about true Christian faith day by day, were the kindest and most loving friends that I ever had. I had no knowledge that led me to believe in the value of prayer, but Ben assured me that it would eventually arise out of experience.

One Sunday morning my first test came. Each week Ben led a visit to the local hospital. About five of us would enter the General Ward. This was a large ward with as many as thirty beds. Our first task was to visit the patients. We passed around hymn sheets and introduced ourselves, though our captive audience was so elderly that they were barely able to do much by way of response. This was my first of many visits to a geriatric ward. After singing a hymn and reading a short passage of scripture, one member of our party would give a short talk based on the subject material of the reading. I waited to see which of my experienced colleagues would be called upon. I was shocked to hear the Rector's announcement. "And now Michael will say a few words for us."

The reading had been the story of the lost sheep from the Gospel of Luke. I have no recollection of what I said on that occasion. At least the subject was familiar to the farmer whose life had changed so dramatically. Perhaps I made the first of my future references to my own 'lost sheep', Aggie, and her lamb.

My new life had begun in earnest and I felt elated and more that a little inebriated with the growing awareness of a spiritual excitement in my life. Both Valerie and I had been so used to the isolation of our much loved Thorn Farm. Now we were submerged in a very different life style. My work with the apprentices and Valerie's as housekeeper to the hostel brought us face to face with a greatly different range of problems.

The apprentices were a mixed bunch of young men. Highly spirited and full of mischief and energy. Their daily, and nightly, adventures ensured a far from peaceful life for the Acting Warden and his wife! One morning the phone rang. It was the Detective Constable Evans from the local police force. "There's a problem Sir. We think that your boys may be able to help us to solve it."

The rush hour traffic had reported a strange happening. A road sign in Farnborough, which normally read 'Welcome to Farnborough', proclaimed in both English and Welsh 'Welcome to Wales'. A call to police on the Welsh border had confirmed that Welsh drivers were being assailed by a new sign that proclaimed 'Welcome to Farnborough'. Both signs had been very professionally erected. The apprentices' Residents Committee denied responsibility but offered to see that the problem was rectified. The following morning both road signs were back in their correct positions! The ingenuity of these young men from the Royal Aircraft Establishment knew no bounds.

One of the occasional happenings was a civil war between the apprentices in Block A with those who occupied Block B. This usually took the form of a water fight. The A's would covertly attack the B's at the dead of night by silently invading Block B armed with buckets of water. Entering bedrooms they would pour icy cold water over the sleeping enemy. Then, making a hasty retreat, they would slosh water mixed with foaming detergent along the corridors. The mess in the morning was indescribable. Valerie would have to placate the cleaning women and help organise the clean ups.

I struggled with how to inflict any punishment or discipline in order to stop this prank. My final resort in the case of serious default was to inform the Director of the R.A.E. This entailed a full official inquiry and could lead to the suspension or expulsion of the offender. This was a course of action to be avoided if at all possible. One night, we received a tip off that there would be a water fight so we decided to wait in ambush. Sure enough the attacking party approached stealthily. The residents from Block B were mounting a counter attack. Shady, lithe figures materialised in the low power lamp light on campus. The attack was soon under way. The boys in Block A were in for a rude awakening.

My intervention was swift. Quite suddenly there was no one to be seen. They had merged into the darkness. I made my way inside and into the corridor. On knocking and entering the bedrooms the residents feigned sleep. Then I noticed the soaking wet bedclothes. Pulling back the bedclothes I saw the soggy sheets and sopping wet apprentices. "Out, Out!" I cried as I distributed mops and towels that had been provided by Valerie's housekeeping department. The boys in Block B were pretended to be innocent but the tell tale trails of water had betrayed them.

It took a great deal of determination to achieve a reasonable standard of clean up. Realising that they would get no more peace or sleep until they had done their best to mop and dry the floors, the miscreants eventually drifted back to their damp bedrooms. Calm was eventually restored.

At the emergency meeting of the Residents Committee the next evening, their Chairman remarked "I thought you were training to enter the Church Mr. Bishop?"

"Yes," I agreed. "That's correct."

"Then you'd be wise to watch your language Sir!" he replied. "You should have heard yourself last night. You'll never be a *real* Bishop if you swear like that!"

I had never been one to use foul language although my work on farms and my time in the Territorial Army had made me aware of the vocabulary. I had been very angry that night. I had spoken the language that I heard all too often as I moved around the campus in the hope that the residents would react to my determination to control the situation. Next day I could not help noticing that an ever growing respect was being afforded me by the apprentices. The hostel was a much happier place. It became easier to instil discipline, and although there was a further water fight a few weeks later it was not on nearly the same scale as in the past.

Back at the church there was excitement concerning the coming of a well known visiting preacher, John V. Taylor, who later became Bishop of Winchester. At that time he was the Africa Secretary for the Church Missionary Society. He was to be with us the following Sunday.

Canon Taylor's sermon highlighted the work of the Christian mission taking place in Africa. He emphasised the need for more members of the church to offer themselves to join in this ministry. Then he mentioned the need for those who had experience of agriculture to go and help develop farming in Kenya. Nurses were also needed. Persons interested were invited to stay on after church for a personal interview with the Canon.

Two of our new friends Pearl and Ken Campbell decided to take up the offer. Pearl was a nurse and Ken was an administrator. "Why don't you stay and see him, Michael?" they suggested. "Perhaps you could help. You've had a farm. You might be just the person he needs!" Unwillingly I yielded to their insistence that I stay to meet with him.

This was a vital decision to have made. John Taylor was an academic and a loving man. He listened to my story patiently. I concluded by saying that perhaps I had been mistaken in seeking to be ordained. Perhaps I should instead be an agricultural missionary. John Taylor explained patiently that the African Governments would not give permission for anyone to enter their country to help with agriculture unless he or she had a degree in agriculture. Once again my lack of education loomed as an obstacle to my future. Perhaps the few 'O' levels I was pursuing would not be good enough! Noticing my despair, John Taylor kindly remarked "Michael, it's getting late now. Would you be able to come to London next Tuesday and have a longer talk with me?" I agreed to do so and an appointment was confirmed.

An Invitation to Oxford

The following Tuesday I made my way to Farnborough railway station. I was on my way to the headquarters of the Church Missionary Society on London's Waterloo Road. To my delight and surprise, Pearl and Ken Campbell were waiting for the train too. We were all responding to Canon John Taylor's invitation to visit with him.

As the train made its way towards London we chatted nervously about the significance of our journey. I recalled how my farming career had started in London at the Ministry of Agriculture. This time I would be visiting the very centre of the Church of England's historic mission to lands and peoples the world over—CMS House. This was to be a journey that would change each one of our lives.

John Taylor's office was small but it suited his kind and humble personality. The Africa Secretary repeated his doubts that I would qualify to undertake missionary work. After a further period of in depth question and answer he came, abruptly, to a decision. "Michael," his eyes seemed to be conducting an X-ray of my feelings and emotions, "I believe that you have been called to be ordained as a priest!" Picking up his telephone he dialled a number. "Ah! David, John Taylor here. I've got a man with me that I'd like you to meet." I left CMS House with an invitation to go to Oxford to meet Canon David Anderson, the Principal of Wycliffe Hall Theological College.

Ken and Pearl made their homeward journey in a deep and awesome mood as well. They were destined to train for missionary service. Their journey led eventually to many years of outstanding missionary service in Nigeria.

The time arrived for me to report to Reading University to take my 'O' level exams. On the appointed day I drove to Reading with my faithful Valerie at my side. As we journeyed she did her best to calm me and to diminish the utter panic that was in danger of taking control of me. I also knew that Ben and the people of the Old Parish Church were upholding me in their prayers. But the terror that stretched back to my years at Langley Place hovered over me like a great storm cloud. If I could not pass the 'O' level exams that awaited me, I knew I would have no opportunity to be accepted into Wycliffe Hall.

Our journey to Reading was hindered by heavy traffic. Then the search for parking eroded more time. I arrived at the Porter's Lodge hot and bothered and with very little time to spare. On inquiring where the exams were being held, I was surprised by the porter's reply. "Tell your youngster it's just down the corridor, first door to the left," he informed me genially.

"It's me that is taking the exams," I stuttered as I dashed down a long corridor and into the lecture room. The room was crowded with teenage boys and girls. There was only one empty desk to be seen which looked extremely small. Watched by many pairs of curious eyes I fitted my bulky form in among the throng of fidgeting scholars. The invigilator ordered silence and the examination papers were distributed. My many hours of study through the evening hours at Farnborough were now to be tested.

My first appraisal of the questions reinforced my inferiority complex. My feeling of terror was heightened. My companions were already studiously at work, heads down, pens active, before I had written a word. As I settled down to work, my memory slowly came to life and the terror abated. I soon became engrossed in the task of tackling the English paper and then the dreaded examination of my religious knowledge.

With the O levels behind me, the next phase of my journey was upon us. Valerie and I were on road once more. This time we were making our way to Oxford. Arriving in Norham Gardens we entered the threshold of Wycliffe Hall. The Principal's Secretary informed us that Canon David Anderson was just down the street. "He's working on his car," she added. "You should go out and introduce yourself."

At the curb side stood a classic, but fast looking car. From under the chassis the sound of scraping and hammering emitted. Protruding from beneath it I saw a pair of legs. They were clad in oily jeans. "Er, excuse me, I'm looking for the Principal," I called out loudly hoping that I could be heard above the sound of the traffic in Banbury Road. A writhing body laboriously extracted itself from under the vehicle. An oily hand was extended to me. My memories of Tom Langley's clean hand, which had so readily grasped my muddy one that rainy years before, came flooding back as I readily responded to his welcome.

"Come along in, both of you. I'll get cleaned up and we can have a chat!" invited the Principal with a bashful smile. David Anderson was a short, rather shabby looking, bespectacled man. He did not fit the image for which my mind had prepared me. I had expected a rather tall, sombre and godly looking person. We were immediately put at ease by his gentle and shy disposition.

Once again my story was listened to intently. I expected to have to negotiate a jungle of difficult questions but to my astonishment he came to a quick decision. "I can offer you a place at Wycliffe, starting at the beginning of the Long Vac term," he announced. It was barely a month ahead.

Our elation quickly diminished. The rules of the College were that married ordinands were to live separate lives from their wives for the first year of their training. Wives, we learned, should reside at least twenty miles distant from their husbands. This condition would be a harsh penalty to pay for a happy and interdependent couple. We had already been married for almost ten years. We had Tim to consider. Would it be right to deprive him of the company of his father for a full twelve months?

The question of tuition fees also arose. We confessed that we had no funds to cover my training expenses. I was advised to contact Hampshire County Education Authority. "You might," David Anderson ventured, "qualify for a Further Education bursary."

A suggestion was made that Valerie and I might like to take a walk in the nearby University Park in order to think things over. It was fine afternoon and the park was beautiful and peaceful. Undergraduates were relaxing under the trees engrossed in their books or wandering quietly along the banks of the River Cherwell. I wondered if I could ever mingle with students among the 'dreaming spires' of Oxford. Could I enter the world of theological study and survive to qualify for a degree? I would have so much ground to make up compared with the other ordinands, most of whom already had degrees or other excellent qualifications. My mind was in turmoil and I was angry. How could the church authorities expect a married couple to live separate lives? It wouldn't be fair to Tim to deprive him of his father's love in the home for a full year. As for Valerie, I wondered how she must be feeling.

My mind went back to our wedding day. The Vicar had proclaimed 'Those whom God hath joined together let no man put asunder'. Those who are responsible for training men to do God's work, I reasoned, were about to separate us! It looked to me as if all our hopes, and the help that had been given to us, was to come to nothing. Perhaps the most sensible action to take would be to pull out and return to my job with the YMCA Community Services in Farnborough. We resolved to return to David Anderson's study and share our feelings.

As we began to communicate our concern David Anderson stopped me with a cautionary lift of his hand. "I've got good news for you," he intervened. "You may not have to worry about it. Wait a few days before you make your decision because the Board and Staff of the College will be holding a meeting which may challenge the arrangement."

We learned later that an ordinand who had begun his training a year earlier had presented the College with a problem. His little boy had been ill and the doctors had been unable to diagnose the cause of his sickness and loss of weight. The child's plight, it was now considered, was due to the fact that he was pining for his father. The Board and Staff of Wycliffe Hall, having been informed of this diagnosis, now voted to change the rules concerning married ordinands. Valerie and I would now be allowed to set up our home nearby in Oxford.

Our first obstacle had been surmounted. The second obstacle was that of finding suitable accommodations. The third was the very major one of finances! My training at Wycliffe Hall would take three years. How could we afford to pay rent for a flat, or buy our food, let alone pay for my tuition? Amazingly these obstacles were very soon dealt with.

The financial problem was met by Hampshire County Council, to whom I shall forever be grateful. They granted me a very generous Further Education bursary which would cover much of the cost of living.

Mrs. Alice Simpson, the widow of D. C. Simpson, a former Dean of Keble College, had contacted the Principal to ask whether he knew of a couple who needed accommodation. She would be glad to meet any suitable couple, especially if the wife of the ordinand would be interested in acting as her companion and housekeeper. She could provide comfortable rooms on the top floor of her house in Banbury Road. It was as if the way ahead was being cleared of numerous rocks and potholes by an unseen hand.

We were invited to tea at 143 Banbury Road, which was just a few minutes walk from Wycliffe Hall. Seldom have we been more nervous. Alice Simpson greeted us at the front door. Her features reminded me of my mother, and her white hair and piercing blue eyes added to the likeness. However, she was much more formal in a Victorian kind of way.

Taking us into her drawing room, she said that she had tea ready. It just needed pouring and bringing in. Valerie, with her future duties in mind, offered to assist. They disappeared to the kitchen together while I took stock of the room. Looking down at me from an old and faded photograph was a stern, but benign looking, clergyman. He wore one of those very wide dog collars which had the effect of making his neck and head resemble that of a tortoise! I later learned that Dean Simpson's nickname at Keble College had been 'Yahweh', the very name given by the Hebrews for God himself.

Valerie returned pushing a tea trolley loaded with cucumber sandwiches. Mrs. Simpson brought in a three-tier cake stand adorned with a selection of tasty looking pastries. "Would you pour for me dear," asked Mrs. Simpson. "My wrists are so weak these days." Valerie picked up the large antique china teapot. As she poured there was a shattering sound. The lid slipped off the pot and scalding tea spilled all over the clean tea cloth, tea trolley and pastries. This was one of those occasions when one wished that the floor would open and swallow you up. Surely this was the end of our hopes for accommodations.

The accident was ably dealt with by Valerie who, as always, showed great courage. A salvaged tea was nervously taken. Mrs. Simpson led us up the stairs to the third floor of the house. "This will be your own private area," she explained. The space was very acceptable and comfortable.

There was one more hurdle to jump. "We have a small son," Valerie announced. "Would you mind having a child in the house?"

Alice Simpson hesitated momentarily. "Bring the little creature in to see me tomorrow morning," she offered.

Tim's visit the next morning was a happy one. "We didn't have a family," Mrs. Simpson informed us as she sat at her fireside. Tim displayed his charm and invented a game of his own using her fireside poker and shovel. "But he's a nice creature," she remarked, adding "I think that we will get on well together." From that moment on, she always referred to Tim as 'The Creature'. A happy friendship had begun. It was destined to develop and mature.

David Anderson invited me to a second interview. This time he was assessing how, considering that I only had two O levels, he could best arrange my tuition. I told him of my great anxiety that I would not be able to survive the course work at Wycliffe Hall. I had no experience of studying at the depth that would be required. I was a slow reader and my memory would probably not be sufficiently good enough to enable me to retain the facts I needed to know.

"Leave that to us, Michael," the Principal replied. He then added, "And have faith that God has called you to do this for him and He will see you through."

Dog Collar and Cassock

Shortly before the end of my stay, Mr. Naylor offered me full time employment as the Warden of the hostel. I was tempted to accept. Both of us were enjoying the work very much. The financial package was also very tempting after all the years of receiving so little reward in the world of farming. The decision was tough to make but Ben Hutchinson had taught us not to take any decisions until we had spent time seeking the Lord's will in prayer. We felt certain that we should press ahead with our plans to follow the path that God had chosen for us.

Shortly before the end of my service with the YMCA at the Royal Aircraft Establishment, I was involved in a near fatal car accident. A member of the hostel staff had been seriously ill and in hospital. As I was on my way home from visiting him one evening, I was driving at the tail end in a fast moving queue of traffic. Realising that the traffic in front of me was stopping, I applied my brakes. My MG Magnet saloon car plunged forward out of control. I was riding on hailstones!

Jumping over the high curb stones, the car mounted a steep bank of grass and turned upward and over onto the roof. Then the car rolled onto its side. I was trapped and could smell fumes of escaping petrol. Fearing that the car would burst into flames, I tried in vain to locate the door handle. But I did not realise that I was feeling for it on the car's inner roof. In naked panic I struggled to find a door or window without avail. I experienced a moment of resignation. Any moment, I thought, I will be enveloped in a ball of fire as the petrol ignites. I thought I was going to perish.

Unexpectedly I felt a draught of fresh air. Looking up I saw the silhouette of a policeman's helmet. "Help," I cried. "I can't find the door."

"It's here, up above you," he told me. "Come straight up." I climbed out into the cold night air. "I never thought I'd find anyone alive in here," he said. "It must be a miracle." As I reflect on all that happened since that evening, I am certain that it was. The police officer called for a taxi and assured me that he witnessed the crash and that I was not to blame. No one else had been involved. Mine had been the last car in the line. As the car lay clear of the highway, it was not holding up any traffic. I made arrangements for the car to be retrieved and journeyed home safely by taxi.

As I was relating my horrific experience to Valerie, she gently removed a small piece of broken glass from inside my ear. The glass was wedged there without having broken my skin. We gave fervent and thankful praise to our Lord and helper for what we felt must have been his intervention and rescue.

During our last months in Farnborough we had been alarmed at times by the extra loud roar of engines down on the runway of the R.A.E.'s airfield. Looking up into the sky one morning, we had been amazed to see what appeared to be a flying bedstead. The plane lifted off the runway in a vertical take off and hovered completely stationary in the sky above us. Many years later we realised that we had been at Farnborough during the development of the then top secret, but now famous, Hawker-Siddeley Harrier 'jump jet' aircraft.

Our farewell from Farnborough was memorable. Ben and Betty Hutchinson and the people of the Old Parish Church launched us towards Oxford with a powerful bombardment of prayer. The sense of the power of the love of God was overwhelming. I owe Ben Hutchinson a great debt of gratitude and thanks. He had tutored me, guided me and trusted me. He gave me the confidence to go forward into my new future.

As their way of saying farewell, the Royal Aircraft Establishment's Apprentices Liaison Committee invited us to take dinner with the senior apprentices. At the appointed hour we were surprised to see a large and polished car at the door. We were ushered into it with touching chivalry. A young apprentice had been delegated to look after Tim for the evening. We were assured that he was an experience baby-sitter! Tim did not seem to object to this arrangement and he waved cheerfully to us out of the window as we drove away.

The evening was memorable and amusing. The restaurant was excellent and no expense was spared. We were told that the apprentices had each contributed towards our spectacular send off. Our minds went back to the hospitality we had experienced at the beginning of our time at the hostel! We were proud that we would be leaving this talented, high spirited and turbulent group of young engineers in a much happier state than that in which we found them.

Our own lives were taking off in a new direction too. The Long Vac Term at Wycliffe Hall was about to begin. The young man who had started work on a farm in 1942 at the tender age of just under 15 was about to join the town and gown community of Oxford College.

Once there, Tim was enrolled at 'Squirrels', a pre-school play group run by a legendary couple of ladies, Miss Bell and Miss Lemon. Tim's teacher was to be

Joan Cobb. When Tim had to face his first day at school, we realised that it was the first time that we had been separated from him for any length of time. His tears evoked ours. We tore ourselves away from the Squirrels and made our way home, realising all the pent up emotions within us.

We held hands and went our way knowing that just as Jesus had once walked with his disciples on the road to Emmaus, he now accompanied each one of us. We learned that prayer was an all day and every day necessity. Prayer was not just an activity to participate in when in special places at certain moments.

Valerie took up and tackled the challenge of trying to minister to Mrs. Simpson's every need with her usual tact and energy. Tim and I, her two 'undergraduates', were constantly coming and going, and often needed feeding and reassuring!

The tensions of the past year had been considerable. Settling down and entering into the academic life of Wycliffe Hall was desperately difficult. That I was ultimately able to do so was due to the understanding and tuition of Canon David Anderson and my tutor, the Reverend Denis Gooderson. I shared a study with Ian Staines, who nursed me through the days, taught me how to prepare my essays and how to glean the salient points from the many books that I had to read and understand. There were times when I despaired of surviving the course. I had a mammoth task before me.

Despite all my worries, I succeeded in passing the General Ordination Examination. On Trinity Sunday in 1965, I knelt amidst the beauty and holiness of Gloucester Cathedral as I presented myself for ordination. The Bishop of Gloucester, The Right Reverend Basil Guy, laid his hands on my head. This act is the crowning moment in the Church's Form and Order for the making of Deacons. The feeling of wonder and utter humility at that moment is beyond my powers of description. The Order of Service in the Book of Common Prayer of 1662, the rite that was in use at that time, is very beautiful.

The Bishop asked me, "Do you trust that you are inwardly moved by the Holy Ghost to take upon you this office and ministration, to serve God for the promoting of His glory, and the edifying of His people?"

I responded to the Bishop's verbal examination in a state of awe. "I trust so."

"Do you think that you are truly called, according to the will of our Lord Jesus Christ, and the due order of this realm, to the ministry of the Church?"

"I think so."

"Do you unfeignedly believe all the Canonical Scriptures of the Old and New Testament, as given of God to convey to us in many parts and in diverse manners the revelation of Himself which is fulfilled in our Lord Jesus Christ?"

"I do."

"Will you diligently read the same unto the people assembled in the church where you shall be appointed to serve?"

"I will."

After the Bishop had further described the duties of a Deacon he asked a final question. "Will you do this gladly and willingly?"

As I gave my final response I felt the weight of the undertaking that lay before me. "I will do so," I affirmed, "The Lord being my helper."

I knew that in spite of my training I was not educated sufficiently or equipped to cope with such a responsibility. I would be utterly dependant upon the wisdom, strength and guidance of the Holy Spirit.

At the moment of my ordination I had offered a prayer that this momentous gift and blessing could be for Valerie too. She has come to share in my ministry, all the way through, with patience and holy love, so this journey is hers as well. None of this could have happened without her.

On Trinity Sunday in 1965 the milking smock of the boy in the mud from a Sussex dairy farm was exchanged for a clergyman's cassock and dog collar. A new life of service undertaken with the authority of Almighty God had taken root.

My ministry began when I was invited to join the Parish team at the churches of St. Mary with St. Matthew in Cheltenham, part of the Diocese of Gloucester. I became Junior Curate under the direction of The Reverend Canon Hugh Evan Hopkins. I worked closely with The Reverend John Andrew, who was Senior Curate, and Patti Schmiegelow, the Parish Worker.

Ian David Bishop, a brother for Timothy by adoption, was born on June 27th, 1965 during our first year in Cheltenham. He was baptised in St. Matthew's, Cheltenham. On the occasion of his first Christmas, he acted the part of the baby Jesus in the parish's crèche, which included live donkeys and sheep! I was Joseph and Valerie was Mary, mother of Jesus.

After a year of serving as Assistant Curate I was ordained a Priest on Trinity Sunday 1966. One day soon afterwards I was visiting a home in a run down block of flats in the town. A very small girl opened the door in response to my timid knock. I was wearing my cassock. She looked me up and down and slammed the door shut. As she ran down the passage inside I could hear her squealing excitedly. Her words made me feel as if my ministry had made a vertical take off with help from the highest level. "Mum, Mum, come quickly. I think it's God at the door!"

Epilogue

Michael stayed in Cheltenham from 1965 until 1968. During this time he also served as the Deputy Director of the Samaritans. Michael's first parish was in the Diocese of Derby. Bishop Geoffrey Allen appointed him as Priest-in-Charge of the parish of the Holy and Undivided Trinity in Edale. Edale is situated in the Peak District of Derbyshire. Michael was Vicar of Edale from 1968 until 1971. During his time in Edale, a barn adjoining the Vicarage was donated to the Church of England by a local landowner, Mrs. Caroline Noel. The barn was converted into an attractive residential centre for young people, to be known as 'Champion House'. Michael became the first Warden of Champion House. Her Royal Highness the Princess Margaret visited Champion House on May 30th, 1969. Since then countless young people from all over the country have been welcomed there.

In 1971, Michael was inducted as Vicar of the parish of St. Cuthbert, in Doveridge, a country parish in the same Diocese. At that time, the village had no more than 350 residents. The building of new estates was already beginning and the influx of many new families brought renewed life to the parish.

The church was attended by the pupils of Brocksford Hall Preparatory School. Their Headmaster, Andrew Robinson, served for a time as Churchwarden. Mr. Peter Jones, a teacher at Thomas Alleynes School in Uttoxeter, joined the church as Lay Reader and later became a non-stipendiary Minister and has served the parish for many years.

The Prison Chaplaincy appointed Michael to serve as Chaplain of Foston Hall, a detention centre for some ninety young offenders in the fifteen to eighteen year old age group. He was also, for a brief time, Priest-in-Charge of the parish of St. Giles in Marston Montgomery.

In 1976, the Bishop of Derby nominated Michael and Valerie, Tim and Ian, to take part in an exchange with the Episcopal Church in America. In May a priest form the Episcopal Church of St. Ambrose, in the Episcopal Diocese of Los Angeles, came to Doveridge and Michael flew out to California with his family. There Michael took over the parish duties in Claremont, about 40 miles east of Los Angeles.

In England, Father John Keester, the Rector of St. Ambrose, and his wife Laurie and their sons Tim and Chris, were welcomed by the congregation at St. Cuthbert's. They have maintained their contact with the parish. Michael's family received a warm welcome from the congregation of St. Ambrose. An additional ministry in Claremont was that of the Episcopal Church's chaplaincy to the Claremont Colleges.

The exchange was arranged by the Venerable Robert Dell, Archdeacon of Derby. Its purpose was to celebrate the bicentennial of the United States of America's Declaration of Independence. Returning home in time for Christmas, the two families resumed their duties in their home parishes.

In 1979, the Bishop family left Doveridge to continue ministering in the parish of Christ Church, Cotmanhay and Shipley. This was a coal mining and steel manufacturing parish. Unemployment was very high and the area was in an extreme state of depression. In addition to his parochial duties, Michael also enjoyed his work as Chaplain of Ilkeston General Hospital.

Valerie, who devoted her life to Michael's ministry and to her two boys, suffered serious injuries when she was run into by a young man astride a powerful motor cycle. She had been distributing posters concerning the programme for Holy Week and Easter. While Tim alerted the emergency services, Ian, who had recently completed a course as in First Aid, bravely staunched the flow of blood from Valerie's wound by using his jacket as a makeshift tourniquet. The family continues to be indebted to the surgeons, doctors and nurses of the Derby Royal Infirmary, and to the parishes and friends who upheld Valerie and her family in prayer. The friendship and practical care of the Reverend Cedric Blakey, who had recently joined the parish as Assistant Curate at the time of Valerie's accident, was greatly appreciated.

In 1981, Father John Keester completed 15 years as the Rector of St. Ambrose and moved on to a new ministry in Bakersfield, California. The Wardens and Vestry of St. Ambrose honoured Michael and Valerie by calling them to serve as their full-time Rector. Ian moved with his parents to California and attended Webb School in Claremont.

Cedric Blakey was greatly respected for the way in which he led the parish of Cotmanhay and Shipley until the appointment of the Reverend Leslie Walters, who succeeded Michael as their Vicar.

Ian completed his education in California receiving a Bachelor's Degree in Economics and now works in the financial services industry. He married in 1989. He and his wife, Julie, have two children, Emma and Owen. They continue to live in California.

Tim remained in England to complete his studies. Tim completed his education and was awarded an Honours Degree in Sociology and a social work qualification. He has mostly worked within mental health services and is now a director of mental health organisation in East London. He shares his life with his partner, Ian Louden, and they live between their London flat and their house in East Anglia.

In May 1989, Michael retired from full-time ministry. He and Valerie returned to live in England. After living in Sussex for a few years, they moved to Norfolk. Here, in the rural village of Colkirk, Michael and Valerie are spending their retirement years. Their home is aptly located across from a farmer's field and just a few houses away from the village church of Saint Mary's.

978-0-595-43224-(

0-595-43224-7

Printed in the United Kingdom
by Lightning Source UK Ltd.
120863UK00002B/175